Polity and Economy

Polity and Economy

With Further Thoughts on the Principles of Adam Smith

Joseph Cropsey

ST. AUGUSTINE'S PRESS
South Bend, Indiana
2001

Manufactured in the United States of America.

1 2 3 4 5 6   07 06 05 04 03 02 01

Library of Congress Cataloging in Publication Data
Cropsey, Joseph.
    Polity and economy : with further thoughts on the
    principles of Adam Smith / Joseph Cropsey.
        p. cm.
    Includes bibliographical references.
    ISBN 1-58731-625-0 (paperbound : alk. paper)
    1. Smith, Adam, 1723–1790. 2. Capitalism – Moral and
    ethical aspects. 3. Free enterprise – Moral and ethical |
    aspects. I. Title.
HB103.S6 C7 2001
330.15'3 – dc21   2001002992

× *The paper used in this publication meets the minimum requirements of
the American National Standard for Information Sciences – Permanence of
Paper for Printed Materials, ANSI Z39.48-1984.*

Table of Contents

Note to the Present Edition

This volume differs from the earlier version in that it contains two essays that were written at a later date. They appear herein as Chapters 4 and 5.

Chicago
July, 2001

Preface

My original research on the present subject was done a number of years ago as I was preparing a doctoral dissertation at Columbia University. I wish to thank Professor Joseph Dorfman for the help he so unstintingly offered at that time.

Only my reluctance to implicate him in the shortcomings of this book prevents me from acknowledging the full measure of my obligation to Professor Leo Strauss of the University of Chicago. His influence upon this study is not to be reckoned in terms of his concurrence with its substance, as to which I cannot testify, or in terms of the credit that this study does to his influence, as to which I can but entertain modest hopes.

I must finally express my gratitude to my parents, to whom this volume is dedicated, for the patient sacrifice which made my training possible.

J. C.

New York
March, 1956

Introduction

One axiomatic premise of this study is that capitalism is that capitalism is an embodiment of Smithian principles. Hence the interpretation of Smith's teaching must also be an interpretation of capitalistic society. A second such premise is that it is at least as likely that Smith had a single view of existence that pervaded both his books as that he had two views of existence which contended in each of his books. Hence the possibility is not excluded that the tension of outlooks reflected in Smith's writings betokens not an inconsistency but an intention. The combined force of these axiomatic premises shapes this study into an attempt to state the ends of Smith's teaching, or his intention, and thus the ends of capitalistic society.

An awareness of even superficial facts concerning Smith and his doctrine inspires a presumption that his economics is not as other men's. Smith was a professor of moral philosophy; and he wrote, in addition to his economic volume, a technical treatise on moral philosophy which was well received by experts. We ought not to be surprised if he conceived his economics within a framework of moral theory according to the fashion of his predecessors since the classical antiquity of Greece. It is part of the purpose of this essay to show that he did so conceive it. As the classic advocate of a system of society, one which, like every other, must be oriented upon a good goal for man compatible with the principles of man's nature, Smith was committed to elucidating matters belonging to moral philosophy. Our task is to follow where he led.

Liberal capitalism depends very much upon the dual idea of free markets and competition. It can do so only because there exists an interpretation of human nature and human life which renders competition and free markets defensible as institutions for men to live by. This is evident from the fact that in other times, and in our own time in other places, those institutions have been rejected as unfit for men to live by, i.e., as inconsistent with man's nature. But doctrines of human nature are inseparable from doctrines of nature in general. We shall therefore have to explore Smith's views of nature and of human nature in order to locate the origins of his economic advocacy.

It is a matter of great interest to us that Smith's view of nature and humanity was not simply Smith's own creation. Indeed a most important fact concerning Smith's teaching is the precision with which it falls into the tradition of modern thought permeated by the spirits of Spinoza and Hobbes. In so far as Smith's underlying views are essentially the propositions of Hobbean and Spinozistic philosophy, his social proposals emerge as the political inferences from the modern view of the whole. That view of the whole takes its departure from an essentially mechanistic, materialistic natural philosophy; from a rejection of the classical doctrine that nature is the form or end rather than the matter of things; or more generally, from a rejection of the traditional teleological view of nature that was oriented upon forms, essences, or Ideas as the highest (truest) categories of being. It proceeds to describe human nature by reference to how men are rather than what man is, i.e., by the "realistic" conception advanced by Machiavelli when he counseled attention to the conduct of men as they "are" rather than to the idea of man's formal excellence. In consequence, humanity, or what is in essence characteristic of mankind, is defined in terms of and by inference from the desire for self-preservation, with the result that it now becomes possible to speak of *the* good which is common to all living things, human and non-human alike. Humanity, or "the human" emerges as an inference from the desire for self-preservation, a desire which is gratified through the working of men's passions. The desire for self-preservation becomes the irreducible, as well as the most compelling, and hence the most dependable, innate activator of the human spirit. In the most important respects, therefore – in respect of the essential human urge to live, and the power to take life – all men are equal. This is the aspect of the Hobbean-Spinozistic doctrine which forms the basis of Smith's theoretical system.

Adam Smith's advocacy of liberal capitalism followed upon a comparison of alternatives, an implicit but nonetheless genuine comparison. For the sake of brevity we may qualify the alternatives as the systems of authoritative virtue and of liberal commerce. By liberal capitalism or the system of liberal commerce is meant the way of life in which commerce is of the essence of society rather than being in any way exceptional or interstitial to it; and in which the good of the whole is supposed to be so intimately related to the prosperity of individuals as such that the latter are left quite free to traffic as they will. In speaking of commerce, I mean what Smith himself meant to convey when he used the term in describing civilized economic life:

> When the division of labour has been once thoroughly established, it is but a very small part of a man's wants which the produce of his own labour can supply. He supplies the far greater part of them by exchanging that surplus part of the produce of his own labour, which is over and above his own consumption, for such parts of the produce of other men's labour as he has occasion for. Every man thus lives by exchanging, or becomes in some measure a merchant, and the society itself grows to be what is properly a commercial society.[1]

Liberal capitalism is contrasted with the social order of the Middle Ages, in which commerce did not exist as a normal or completely legitimate activity; and with authoritative mercantilism, which acknowledged the legitimacy of commerce but distinguished between the mere prosperity of individuals and the well-being of society, and hence constrained the former, by inhibiting competition, for the sake of the latter.

Smith's final advocacy of liberal capitalism gains in

---

1   *Wealth of Nations*, Bk. I, Ch. IV, p. 37.

stature for its issuance from a comparison. At least he had not been made ignorant of alternatives by his environment. Yet this comparison, as all others must do, meant the weighing and measuring of advantages against disadvantages. Serious comparison would be meaningless because unnecessary, were there not advantages and disadvantages on both sides. And so, at an hour when these least deserve to be intruded upon the mind, we are obliged to disinter Smith's adverse reflections upon our way of life.

The times have almost made us believe that a critique of commercial society must emanate either from the Right or from the Left. We have almost forgotten those reflections upon the commercial principle which antedate Left, Right, and capitalism alike by comparable periods. Those critical reflections, originating in classical times, issued neither from the Left nor from the Right, but rather from Above. Adam Smith's critique of liberal capitalism is undertaken from a quasi-classical standpoint, and gives utterance to a dying vestige of antiquity in his thought which raised his criticism above Right and Left, had such dimensions been known to him. It goes without saying that we must be vigilant to prevent the twentieth century from appearing in our eye as we behold the eighteenth. Specifically, we must be scrupulous not to distort the orientation of Smith's critique of the commercial principle lest we seriously misconstrue his largest purposes.

The immediate practical value of a reexamination of Smith's doctrine is in part suggested by the foregoing remarks on the relation between a system of society and the theoretical principles that underlie it: if we wish to understand our way of life, we must first see the basis upon which it rests. Much of the present century has been, and doubtless much of its remainder will be given its character by the effort of liberalism to preserve itself. That effort can succeed only if it issues from a general determination to preserve the present way of life; but such a determination is never to be looked for without a distinct and honest understanding of the good which is sought through the means of liberal capitalism. I believe that we can help ourselves to such an understanding by a study of Smith's doctrines. On these lines it will be argued that Smith advocated capitalism because it makes freedom possible – not because it *is* freedom. The distinction is of some importance. To argue that capitalism is freedom would put one in the position of affirming that the chief blessing of liberalism is that it leaves everyone free to become prosperous however he sees fit. Now capitalism doubtless does leave everyone free in this way; but it is a freedom that by its nature must have ambiguous results for the majority of mankind. Smith himself supposed that, in any prosperous society, for every rich man there must be five hundred poor.² Can the five hundred be induced to adore freedom if freedom means the absence of legal inhibitions in the way of any citizen wishing to mine diamonds on a capital of one thousand dollars? As well claim that we are free and should be grateful for it because the law does not prevent our free ascent to the moon. Such a misconstruction of the freedom associated with capitalism is what has as much as anything beclouded opinion. It has prepared the way for the idea that freedom is a mockery because, for multitudes, opulence does not come of it. Related to that misconstruction is the absurdity that a man constrained by circumstances and a man restrained by the law are unfree in the same sense; as if mortal men might ever be unconstrained by circumstances. Smith did not, of course, belittle the freedom of everyone to occupy himself as he wished and might, wheresoever he could and in whose employ he could find work. But he thought even more of the principle that where the people are impelled from within, viz. by their interested passions, to do the things needful for social existence, they will not have to be impelled from without, or bound to their duty by powerful civil and ecclesiastical masters. Let it be generally understood that liberal capitalism was regarded by one of its architects as the common prop of two entities which had never before stood simultaneously – civil and ecclesiastical freedom – and liberalism will appear in a clearer light than it has often done.

There is another way of describing the good that may be had from a reexamination of Smith's doctrine: It causes us,

---

23 Ibid., Bk. V, Ch. I, Pt. II, p. 710.

and at the same time assists us, to revert to the first principles of our society in company with a spirit undistracted by the preconceptions and issues of this century. In one sense liberalism has succeeded so well that we have lost sight of some of its problematic aspects. We have too much ceased to question the practical possibility of freedom as we know it, perhaps because the apparent success of liberalism seems to have done away with the question. Ceasing to question, we have ceased to consider that freedom exists upon a substructure of necessary conditions. We recapture some sense of this when we recur to the literature of a time when modern liberalism was viewed as an experiment. That time is not remote from us. The nobility of the Gettysburg Address is so moving that it sometimes blinds us to the theme upon which Lincoln spoke: can a nation conceived in liberty and dedicated to the proposition that all men are created equal, long endure. Abraham Lincoln solved the problem in a political way by vindicating the principle that freedom is not introspective, cannot deliberate its own existence, and does not include the freedom to destroy itself. A nation so conceived and so dedicated depends for its endurance upon its vigor (and its prudence) in suppressing the element of freedom that would divert the nation into slavery. But something more is needed than a principle that makes it illegal for freedom to murder itself. What is needed at the very minimum is a feasible and satisfactory substitute for strong authority, which is yet compatible with good order and good living in society. Whether, and wherein, such a substitute exists, is the lasting problem of freedom. The existence of this problematic aspect of liberal life is brought to our attention by Smith's effort to cope with it; and we profit as greatly by being reminded of the problem as we do by the answer proffered, namely the passionate pursuit of interest under the aegis of free competition.

CHAPTER I
THE GENERAL FOUNDATION
OF SMITH'S SYSTEM

The existence of the *Theory of Moral Sentiments* testifies that Adam Smith's view included more than is contained in political economy alone. Although it might be extravagant to place Adam Smith in the rank of those philosophers who had a conception of the whole of being, it is entirely proper to say that his conclusions as to the character of human life do rest upon discernible first principles with which he had a conscious concern. True it is that he is best remembered for his propositions on economy and social organization; yet those propositions must remain as detached and unsupported dogmas unless they harmonize with some rational view of the principles of existence in general. It is in the *Theory of Moral Sentiments* that Adam Smith in part states and in part implies those first principles which, when they are regarded in their mutual relation, form the theoretical system upon which his advocacy of commercial society rests. Our present task is to try to understand that system for the sake of the social doctrine in which it culminates.

Each science, and every scientific doctrine, depends for its soundness upon the success with which it identifies the nature of its object. And the nature or essential principle of its object cannot well be separated from the nature or principle of the whole or of nature simply. Indeed, if we thoroughly understood the meaning of nature in general, we should in many cases find that we understood the nature of "each thing" as well as of "all things." Thus if we were to mean by nature, "the principle of motion in the whole," we should certainly mean by the nature of any object the principle of motion in that object. Or if we were to regard nature at large as meaning the material components of the universe, we could scarcely escape meaning by the nature of a particular object *its* material components.

Of Adam Smith it may be said that he enunciated a broad system relating to human life, a system which proceeds from a recognizable view of human nature. Smith too realized that the meaning of human nature is inseparable from the meaning of nature simply; and that the full meaning of a social system that grows out of an interpretation of human nature must await an exposition of nature in general for its full expression. These causes by themselves would justify if not compel us to begin with Smith's view of nature at large. In addition, it happens that Smith never referred to his system of social proposals as capitalism, free-enterprise, or *laissez-faire*, the terms by which we now know them, but rather as "the natural system of perfect liberty and justice" and "the system of natural liberty,"[1] which he surely did for reasons connected with his view of nature and its relation to systems of polity. Let us then turn to consider Smith's conception of nature simply.

The essential ingredient of Smith's doctrine of nature appears in the important note which follows Chapter V, Section 1, Part II of the *Theory of Moral Sentiments*.

There Smith writes:

> . . . self-preservation, and the propagation of the species, are the great ends which Nature seems to have proposed in the formation of all animals. Mankind are endowed with a desire of those ends, and an aversion to the contrary; with a love of life, and a dread of dissolution; with a desire of the continuance and perpetuity of the species, and with an aversion to the thoughts of its entire extinction. But though we are in this manner endowed with a very strong desire of those ends, it has not been entrusted to the slow and uncertain determinations of our reason to

1   *Wealth of Nations*, Bk. IV, Ch. VII, Pt. III, p. 606; Bk. IV, Ch. IX, p. 687.

find out the proper means of bringing them about. Nature has directed us to the greater part of those by original and immediate instincts. Hunger, thirst, the passion which unites the two sexes, the love of pleasure, and the dread of pain, prompt us to apply those means for their own sakes, and without any consideration of their tendency to those beneficent ends which the great Director of nature intended to produce by them.[2]

It appears that, by genus, nature is an internal principle, or an internal impulsion in virtue of which all living (scil. moving) things act or move as they do. Defined in terms of its end, nature is the principle that aims at the everlasting preservation of all living things, individual and specific. The discussion in the *Theory of Moral Sentiments* applies only to animals, including man, but in his essay on "The History of the Ancient Physics," Smith extends his doctrine to all things. He refers to the universal mind "who governs the whole by general laws, directed to the conservation and prosperity of the whole," and to "the Universe . . . as a coherent system, governed by general ends, *viz.*, its own preservation and prosperity, and that of all the species that are in it."[3] Certainly as to living things, nature is the internal principle that establishes life as the supreme desideratum. There being no mention of any end beyond life, or of anything to which the possession of life is supposed to contribute, we must say that life appears as the highest good or the thing which is desired for its own sake and not for the sake of anything else.

What Smith means by self-preservation and the propagation of the species is the infinite protraction of what was traditionally called the life of nutrition and generation. The biological functions which comprise life so defined were recognized

---

2   See also *Theory of Moral Sentiments*, Pt. II, Sect. II, Ch. III, p. 87. All references to the Theory of Moral Sentiments, and to all other essays by Smith, pertain to the edition reprinted by the Liberty Fund.

3   "History of the Ancient Physics," pp. 391–2, *loc.cit.*

as "motions" in remote antiquity and in modern times alike.[4] Smith himself so names them, referring to the operations of the organs as "motions."[5] The purpose of nature, in so far as animals are concerned, is, then, to perpetuate or conserve the form of motion which is biological life.[6] All of this is, of course, compatible with what is usually described as the mechanistic character of Smith's doctrine.

---

4   Cf. Hobbes, *Leviathan*, Vol. III of the English Works of Thomas Hobbes, ed. Molesworth, London, 1841, Ch. 6, p. 38: "There be in animals, two sorts of *motions* peculiar to them: one called *vital*; begun in generation, and continued without interruption through their whole life; such as are the *course* of the *blood*, the *pulse*, the *breathing*, the *concoction*, *nutrition*, *excretion*, etc. to which motions there needs no help of imagination: the other is *animal motion*, otherwise called *voluntary motion*; as to *go*, to *speak*, to *move* any of our limbs, in such manner as is first fancied in our minds."

5   "But in these, as in all such objects, (*viz.*, the organs) we still distinguish the efficient from the final cause of their several motions and organizations. The digestion of the food, the circulation of the blood, and the secretion of the several juices which are drawn from it, are operations all of them necessary, etc." *Theory of Moral Sentiments*, Pt. II, Sect. II, Ch. III, p. 87.

6   The relation of Smith to the main line of 16th- and 17th-century thought in respect of this important principle is quite clear. In *Leviathan*, Ch. 15, Hobbes writes, "The Law of Nature [comprises] . . . those rules which conduce to the preservation of man's life on earth." Also Spinoza, *Ethics* (London, 1883, tr. Elwes), in Bk. III, Prop. VI: "Each thing, in so far as it is in itself, endeavors to persevere in its being;" Prop. VII: "The effort by which each thing endeavors to persevere in its own being is nothing but the actual essence of the thing itself;" and Prop. IX: "The mind, both in so far as it has clear and distinct ideas, and in so far as it has confused ideas, endeavors to persevere in its being for an indefinite time, and is conscious of this effort." Carrying further the argument from self-preservation, Smith writes that "Death is the greatest evil which one man can inflict upon another." (*Theory of Moral Sentiments*, Pt. II, Sect. II, Ch. II, p. 84). Hobbes (*Leviathan*, Ch. 27) writes, "To kill against the law is a greater crime than any other injury, life preserved." Contrast Plato, *Crito*, 44D.

But it is also true then that life as such can be described as a kind of motion in a larger sense, as the sum of the motions of the individual in a lifetime. Mere life, or life as such, is in effect protracted vital motion, or the functioning of the organs for years or forever, and it can indeed be conceived as having no intelligible purpose other than its own conservation. Designating life as motion indeed distinguishes it from "activity," which is a form of doing that terminates in an "actualization" or true end.

As for Smith, however, we may say that the profoundest governing principle of being is directed to the "purpose" of preserving that form of motion which, in the case of animals, is called life. The purpose of nature is endless existence or vital motion as a thing good in itself.

Human nature is to be understood as that principle in virtue of which man seeks above all else the continuance of his vital motion, or life. It is to be noted that self-preservation or the conservation of life predominates, and can thus be said to be an end, in the sense that it is what is desired above all other things, or in other words it is that for which all human beings have by nature a supervening appetite.[7] And in addition to their being drawn toward the supreme end by appetite, their nature is such that the means to that end will be the means suggested to them by appetite, passion, or instinct.[8] This must be so, we are told, because, of the two human functions which might direct action, namely reason and passion, the former is unsuited to the task of direction. A theme of the utmost impor-

---

7   "With regard to all those ends which, upon account of their peculiar importance, may be regarded, if such an expression is allowable, as the favourite ends of nature, she has constantly in this manner . . . endowed mankind with an appetite for the end which she proposes . . . ." Pt. II, Sect. I, Ch. V, p. 77n

8   Nature has "not only endowed mankind with an appetite for the end which she proposes, but likewise with an appetite for the means by which alone this end can be brought about, for their own sakes, and independent of their tendency to produce it." *Ibid.*

tance, which recurs[9] in the *Wealth of Nations* as in the *Theory of Moral Sentiments* and elsewhere, is the inadequacy of reason to the furtherance of the principal objects of existence. Nature causes men to seek their good by making their good attractive to their passions. If it did otherwise, a creature of man's feeble powers would neither see the end nor the best means to it, nor be able to rule himself well enough to attain it, and his existence, while it endured, would be a contradiction of nature itself as the principle of the conservation of life.

It will be observed that two separate ideas are contained in the foregoing proposition, namely (1) that reason cannot be relied upon to discern the means and the end; and (2) that reason cannot procure adoption of the best means to the end, i.e. cannot govern conduct. Much of what ensues in this chapter will be addressed to the problems which arise around these two central propositions relating to the power of reason.

* * *

The unreliability of reason to discern the natures of things might be ascribed to one, or both, of two large causes: the radical impotence of the mind and its auxiliaries; and the nonexistence of natures to be known. We may speak of both possibilities almost at one time.

Adam Smith inferentially rejected the traditional view of the senses as the indispensable adjuncts of reason, the faculties by the cooperation of which the whole may be made accessible to reason. He regarded them as imperfect aids to comprehension. Professing himself the protagonist of Berkeley on the sense of vision,[10] Smith reasons that the purpose of nature in bestowing upon man the crucial sense of sight was to assist in the practical affairs of life. Thus there are two worlds, a tangible world and a visible world, which "bear no sort of resem-

---

9   E.g., *Wealth of Nations*, Bk. V, Ch. I, Pt. III, Art. II, pp. 769, 803; *Theory of Moral Sentiments*, Pt. II, Sect. I, Ch. V, p. 77n; Pt. VI, Sect. III, p. 237.

10   Adam Smith, "Of the External Senses," in *Essays on Philosophical Subjects* (Indianapolis: Liberty Fund, 1982) p. 148.

blance to each other."[11]The visible world appears to us as a perspective image upon a plane surface, and the sense of vision is the faculty by which we solve the problem of the spatial relation to each other and to ourselves of tangible objects at a distance. The faculty of vision is such that it solves the problem with an accuracy that is in direct proportion to the nearness of the objects to ourselves. We are accurately informed of the relations of things close to us, i.e., the things touching our existence most nearly, such as the objects over which we might stumble and thus endanger our lives. We are least accurately informed of the relations of remote things like the fixed stars; but "the most precise knowledge of the relative situation of such objects could be of no other use to the enquirer than to satisfy the most unnecessary curiosity."[12] From this set of considerations we may draw two related conclusions: First, the faculty which once was regarded as the main aid to the reason in knowing the essences of things or their internal being, is by Smith regarded as the means for knowing rather the relations of things to each other, i.e., their external relations. And second, the purpose of nature in affording vision was not to assist the reason towards knowledge but to promote life as such as the supreme end:

> The benevolent purpose of nature in bestowing upon us the sense of seeing, is evidently to inform us concerning the situation and distance of the tangible objects which surround us. Upon the knowledge of this distance and situation depends the whole conduct of human life, in the most trifling as well as in the most important transactions. Even animal motion depends upon it; and without it we could neither move, nor even sit still, with complete security.[13]

---

11   Ibid., p. 150.

12   Ibid., p. 151.

13   Ibid., p. 156. Cf. Aristotle, *De Anima*, 435b19 ff.: "All the senses other than touch are necessary to animals, as we have said, not for their being, but for their well-being. Such, e.g., is sight . . . ."

We may summarize the argument to this point approximately as follows: Nature provides man with imperfect perceptions of the tangible world, with the inevitable result that he can reason only imperfectly concerning the nature of things or what they really are. The faculty of reason leans upon an aid which was prepared by nature to assist not reason but appetite, specifically the appetite for life as such; and as a result, useful knowledge but not real knowledge is the most that man can aspire to.

From this it would follow that a life spent in the pursuit of "real knowledge" (which is the only knowledge properly so-called, Smith's "useful knowledge" being a more or less inaccurate impression) would be a life devoted to pursuing a chimera. The real nature of things having been placed beyond the combined reason and sense perception of man, to set real knowledge as the goal of life would be to waste life entirely. As we should have expected, Adam Smith explicitly joins the ranks of those who rejected the traditional principle that the contemplative was the best way of life for man. Philosophy, the object and culmination of the contemplative life, anciently regarded as the most serious end of man, is classed by Smith with pictures and poems as of too little account to cause dispute:

> Though you despise that picture, or that poem, or even that system of philosophy, which I admire, there is little danger of our quarrelling upon that account. Neither of us can reasonably be much interested about them. They ought all of them to be matters of great indifference to us both; so that, though our opinions may be opposite, our affections may still be very nearly the same.[14]

Perhaps Smith's most general statement of the rejection of contemplation as the highest human possibility is the following:

> To man is allotted a much humbler department, but one much more suitable to the weakness of his pow-

---

14 *Theory of Moral Sentiments*, Pt. I, Sect. I, Ch. IV, p. 19. "Affections" is synonymous with "passions."

ers, and to the narrowness of his comprehension; the
care of his own happiness, of that of his family, his
friends, his country: that he is occupied in contem-
plating the more sublime, can never be an excuse for
his neglecting the more humble department; . . . The
most sublime speculation of the contemplative
philosopher can scarce compensate the neglect of the
smallest active duty.[15]

We may interpret to the same effect Smith's several references
to the antithesis of nature and philosophy, as for example,
"That kings are servants of the people, to be obeyed, resisted,
deposed, or punished, as the public conveniency may require,
is the doctrine of reason and philosophy; but it is not the doctrine of Nature."[16] Also, "The reasonings of philosophy, it may
be said, though they may confound and perplex the understanding, can never break down the necessary connection
which Nature has established between causes and their
effects."[17] The latter passage asserting (as the former implies)
the impotence of reason against natural links of cause and
effect, goes beyond the commonplace that we cannot alter the
order of nature by reasoning about it. If understood in the context of Smith's attribution of natural preeminence to the passions as causes, it signifies the intransigence of the passions to
merely rational governance. Fuller examination of this point
will be reserved for the treatment of Smith's views on moral
education, to which it properly pertains.[18]

According to this teaching concerning knowledge and
truth, man is by his nature constituted to seek the preservation
of life as the object of life, and the passions rather than the
intellect are what perceive this and execute it. The manner in
which they execute it is yet to be stated, but whatever the manner might be, life lived under the aegis of the passions is life

15   Ibid., Pt. VI, Sect. II, Ch. III, p. 237.
16   Ibid., Pt. I, Sect. III, Ch. II, p. 53.
17   Ibid., Pt. VII, Sect. II, Ch. I, p. 293.
18   See below, pp. 27 ff.

according to nature; the life of contemplation is not according to nature. Corresponding to the contemplative life is the active exercise of the intellect; corresponding to the life according to nature is performance of "active duty." The latter so far exceeds the former in importance that "the most sublime speculation of the contemplative philosopher can scarce compensate the neglect of the smallest active duty." Excellence in contemplation must therefore be inferior to excellence in the performance of active duty. This doctrine we may translate into conventional terms by speaking of it as the assertion of the superiority of moral to intellectual virtue. In this connection it is noteworthy that the *Theory of Moral Sentiments,* Smith's formal statement on moral philosophy, is entirely a discussion of moral virtue and contains no systematic treatment of or reference to intellectual excellence except, as will be discussed later, in the case of a prudence deliberately shrunken in scope from its traditional estate. Applied to the problem of what is the right rule of life for man, Smith's principle of the relation of moral and intellectual virtue leads to the conclusion that man should live for active utility, i.e., service, and that the perfection of a human being is ultimately intelligible in terms of doing good to others. Needless to say, everything then comes to depend upon the meaning of "good." In effect the answer to this has already been given when we showed that, for Smith, the natural end of life (i.e., the most intensely desired thing of all) is the preservation of life. "Doing good to others" means somehow assisting them to what will conduce to life; and service or utility is therefore to be understood as doing those things which directly or indirectly conduce to the end of life.

Illustrative of this conception of Smith's is his account of the irregularity of nature that leads man to commend and blame his fellows on account of the issue rather than the motive of their behavior.

> Man was made for action, and to promote by the exertion of his faculties such changes in the external circumstances both of himself and others, as may seem most favourable to the happiness of all. . . . The man who has performed no single action of importance . . .

can be entitled to demand no very high reward, even though his inutility should be owing to nothing but the want of an opportunity to serve. We can still ask him, What have you done? What actual service can you produce, etc.[19]

The natural predominance of service, or utility to life as the excellence of man is illustrated by, and also helps explain, an important problem raised in the *Theory of Moral Sentiments*, namely, What is the order in which individuals and society are by nature recommended to our good offices? The answer in general is that nature has disposed us toward individuals and societies in the order of their proximity to ourselves; so that we wish most strongly to do the best first for ourselves, then for our immediate families, then for remoter relatives, next for strangers; and we naturally desire the well-being of our own society first, of our own order of society first, and so on. The rule is proximity, not desert. Since the individuals and societies nearest us are those upon whose well-being we can have the greatest practical effect, nature in substance disposes man to seek the good (i.e., preservation) of those individuals and societies which he is best able to serve.[20] That this is not an unimportant aspect of Smith's teaching will be recognized from the fact that his discussion of these matters commences with the crucial observation that "every man . . . is first and principally recommended to his own care; and every man is certainly, in every respect fitter and abler to take care of himself than of any other person."[21]

Attention must be given to Smith's precise expression of

---

19   *Theory of Moral Sentiments*, Pt. II, Sect. III, Ch. III, p. 106. Much has been written on the conflict between the moral principles of capitalism and of (at least primitive) Christianity. On the extremely important point of the relation between moral and intellectual virtue, however, and in much of what it implies, they unite to confront their common antagonist, the morality of classical antiquity.

20   Ibid., Pt. VII, Sect. II, Chs. I and III, *ad fin.*

21   Ibid., Pt. VI, Sect. II, Ch. I. The same observation is made in Pt. II, Sect. II, Ch. II.

this seemingly familiar idea. "Every man is fitter to take care of himself than of any other person" is not identical with the more common "every man is fitter to take care of himself than any other person is fit to take care of him." The former means, A can take care of himself better than he can take care of B. The latter means, B can take care of himself better than A can take care of him. The failure of the two to coincide as general propositions may be seen if it be supposed that A is wise and B is foolish. Their compatibility with each other and with reason would be assured by the extinction of the difference between wisdom and folly. The extinction is accomplished, as will be seen, not absolutely but as far as necessary, by the principle that each man is wise in his own affairs. This will be discussed later as the modern substitution of Little Prudence for Superior Prudence in the calendar of virtues.[22]

It goes without saying that Smith did not assume all men to be perfectly wise in their own affairs. The *Wealth of Nations* is replete with instances of individuals misunderstanding their interest. To the extent to which individuals fail to judge their interest correctly, or ignore the facts about it, they are not in a position to make strictly "sane" decisions. In so far as this is true, and to the extent to which circumstances render misjudgment and ignorance inevitable, the success of the liberal system at large requires some dependence upon the "wisdom of government" to indicate, and even to make, sane decisions for the people. Smith's discussion of the Ayr Bank and of banking generally, in Book II of the *Wealth of Nations,* illustrates this. In general, his assignment of functions to government, *laissez faire* only apparently to the contrary notwithstanding, becomes more intelligible in this light than it does by interpreting him as an eighteenth century harbinger of peculiarly twentieth century liberalism.

The argument to this point may be gathered together and stated briefly as follows: The definition of nature as the principle of the preservation of life for its own sake leads directly to the conclusion that existence according to nature means to

---

22   See below, pp. 47 ff.

promote the preservation of the creatures of nature, or to "serve" them. Admittedly each one must serve himself first, but so completely does preservation pervade nature that it is impossible to serve oneself exclusively. In a well-known passage, Smith says:

> [The rich] consume little more than the poor, and in spite of their natural selfishness and rapacity, though they mean only their own conveniency . . . they divide with the poor the produce of all their improvements. They are led by an invisible hand to make nearly the same distribution of the necessaries of life, which would have been made, had the earth been divided into equal portions among all its inhabitants, and thus without intending it, without knowing it, advance the interest of the society, and afford means to the multiplication of the species.[23]

The natural function par excellence is service or utility to life, and human perfection must therefore coincide with the best or perfect mode of active service to life. But this is sovereign moral (social) virtue.

But what exactly is the nature of those virtues which comprise the excellence of mankind? Smith declares that "to feel much for others and little for ourselves, that to restrain our selfish, and to indulge our benevolent affections, constitutes the perfection of human nature."[24] Perhaps the outstanding implication of this passage is that the perfection of human nature is "feeling" or "affection," both terms being synonymous with emotion, sentiment, or passion; and more exactly, that the perfection of human nature consists of a combination of humanity and self-command, or "fellow-feeling" and "self-regard." The meaning of this is what we must now attempt to explore.

Supposing the truth of the venerable proposition that virtue must exist either as faculty, passion, or disposition,

---

23 *Theory of Moral Sentiments*, Pt. IV, Ch. I, pp. 304. The fuller meaning of this passage is discussed below, pp. 30–31.

24 Ibid., Pt. I, Sect. I, Ch. V, p. 25.

Smith seems to take the stand that virtue corresponds most closely with passion. This conclusion is suggested not only by the passage cited immediately above, and by the very title "Theory of Moral Sentiments," but also by those elements of his system which are to be described next, namely, the criteria of human excellence and how they come to be and to be known.

Human beings are moved to action by their passions, and upon the moving passion the whole virtue or vice of the resulting action depends.[25] Thus virtue inheres in passions which embody propriety and merit. What can we learn concerning these two conditions of virtue, propriety and merit?

Every human being has the power to feel the passions of those other beings who come under his observation. The man who observes the joy of another will himself experience joy, and the spectator of grief or of fear will himself feel some measure of grief or fear. When the spectator finds that the joy, grief, or other passion which he observes was excited by a cause which moves him to the identical measure of passion that he sees displayed, he is said to sympathize with and approve the actions flowing from those passions, and to regard the actions as virtuous. The spectator was able to sympathize and approve as he did because the patient modulated his passion down to the level at which the spectator could enter into it. This done, the spectator is struck by the fitness of the patient's passionate response to the outward stimulus; and the passion itself is said to be marked by propriety, and hence by virtue, if all spectators might feel the same degree of passion, hence sympathy, and finally approbation. The propriety of a passion and the virtue of the resulting action are therefore known by and indeed established through a congruity or concord of the passions of the agent and the passions of all men.[26]

---

25   Ibid., Pt. I, Sect. I, Ch. III, p. 18; Pt. II, Sect. I, Intro., p. 67; Pt. II, Ch. II, Sect. II, p. 84; Pt. III, Ch. V, p.162.

26   Our fluctuation between the use of "patient" and "agent" to describe the same person in a given situation is not the result of a terminological confusion in Smith, but follows from his para-

If a man be moved by passion to act toward another with benevolence, gratuitously doing him some good, the beneficiary will or ought to feel gratitude toward his benefactor. And if gratuitous harm be done, the injured one will feel resentment. If the good was gratuitous, i.e., not owing but offered "of grace" or benevolently, or if the injury was gratuitous, i.e., not warranted by a like previous injury on the other hand; then the action will be said to be marked by merit or by demerit, as the case might be. The agent's action will be approved as meritorious if every spectator can enter into the beneficiary's gratitude, which will be possible only if the agent acted with propriety as already defined. The agent's action will be disapproved as having demerit if it moves the one acted upon to resentment with which the whole world would sympathize. In fine, if a man acts so that every spectator[27] would approve his conduct, then he has acted virtuously. The very words right and wrong have and can have no other meaning than what by our emotions we sympathize with and approve, or fail to sympathize with and thus disapprove.

> When we judge in this manner of any affection as proportioned or disproportioned to the cause which excites it, it is scarce possible that we should make use of any other rule or canon but the correspondent affection in ourselves. If, upon bringing the case home to our own breast, we find that the sentiments which it gives occasion to, coincide and tally with our own, we necessarily approve of them as proportioned and suitable to their objects; if otherwise, we necessarily disapprove of them, as extravagant and out of proportion.

> Every faculty in one man is the measure by which he judges of the like faculty in another. I judge of your

doxical principle that to act means first to have been acted upon, or that passion is the root of action.

27 "Every indifferent person," *Theory of Moral Sentiments*, Pt. I, Sect. I, Ch. V, p. 24: "every reasonable man," Ibid., Pt. II, Sect. I, Ch. II, p. 70; "every impartial spectator," Pt. II, Sect. II, Ch. I, p. 78, etc.

sight by my sight, of your ear by my ear, of your reason by my reason, of your resentment by my resentment, of your love by my love. I neither have, nor can
have, any other way of judging about them.[28]

That virtue and vice are simply derivative from our approbation and disapprobation appears likewise from the proposition that "the different passions or affections of the human
mind which are approved or disapproved of, appear morally
good or evil"[29] and indeed are the only origin of the appearance of moral good or evil, since, as Smith wrote, "The very
words right, wrong, fit, improper, graceful, unbecoming,
mean only what pleases or displeases those [moral] faculties."
But the moral faculties are pleased only by the mechanical
process of sympathetic approbation in the form of "pleasure."[30] This is made clear by Smith when he writes,

nothing can be agreeable or disagreeable for its own
sake, which is not rendered such by immediate sense
and feeling. If virtue, therefore, in every particular
instance, necessarily pleases for its own sake, and if
vice as certainly displeases the mind, it cannot be reason, but immediate sense and feeling, which thus rec-
onciles us to the one, and alienates us from the other.

Pleasure and pain are the great objects of desire and
aversion; but these are distinguished, not by reason,
but by immediate sense and feeling. If virtue, therefore, be desirable for its own sake, and if vice be, in the
same manner, the object of aversion, it cannot be reason which originally distinguishes those different
qualities, but immediate sense and feeling.[31]

That is to say, the distinction between virtue and vice or
between right and wrong conduct is the product of a purely
mechanical process – a process not guided by free under-

---

28 Ibid., Pt. I, Sect. I, Ch. III, p. 18.
29 Ibid., Pt. VII, Sect. III, Ch. III, p. 325.
30 Ibid., Pt. III, Ch. V, p. 165.
31 Ibid., Part VII, Sect. III, Ch. II, p. 320.

standing of intrinsic goodness or badness, but by sympathetic reaction to passion.

In the light of this doctrine it appears that sympathy as the basis of moral judgment is entirely compatible with an advocacy of acquisitive commercialism, though this is sometimes doubted. It is perfectly possible to act at the behest of the selfish passions in a way with which all spectators may sympathize, as Smith clearly affirmed. When Smith constructed his theory upon the foundation of propriety, he fashioned a moral system which, by the formalism of its criterion, could and did embrace every human inclination, provided only that it was manifested in accordance with "propriety." Another way of putting this would be by saying that there is room among the excellences for every passion; and that it is the intensity with which the passion is manifested rather than the nature of the passion, which affects its reception as virtuous or vicious. Sympathy, therefore, must not be mistaken for benevolence.[32]

This account of the moral criterion raises a number of questions into which we must now briefly enter. In the first place, Smith said nothing concerning the means by which the passions are communicated from one being to another – a communication which is indispensable to the sympathy process.[33] However, although as Morrow says, " . . . [Smith] had no epistemological theory with which [his psychology] had to be related," Smith did have a view of nature and of life

---

32 Ibid., Part VI, Sect. I, pp. 215–6. Cf. G. R. Morrow, "The Significance of the Doctrine of Sympathy in Hume and Adam Smith," in the *Philosophical Review*, vol. XXXII, pp. 72–3. See O. H. Taylor, "Economics and the Idea of *Jus Naturale*," in *Quarterly Journal of Economics*, vol. XLIV, p. 234.

33 Cf. G. R. Morrow, "Significance of the Doctrine of Sympathy," p. 69: "Sympathy, or this participation in the feelings of others, is the basis of the moral life. Adam Smith made no attempt to explain the psychological operation of this principle in the individual mind; he had no epistemological theory with which it had to be related." See also Leslie Stephen, *English Thought in the Eighteenth Century*, vol. II, p. 71: "Smith's ingenuity in tracing the workings of the mechanism of human nature is so marked and

with which his psychology had to be related. As we have seen, Smith equated life to motion. The reduction of life to motion implies the reduction of the living thing to the moving thing, to what is capable of motion, to matter. This fact provides us with a clue to the probable outline of Smith's psychology. I shall venture to suggest through the following analogy what that outline might well be if Smith's psychology is to be consistent with his reduction of life to motion and his parallel teaching concerning the origin of action in passion.

Let us represent the soul by a tuning fork, i.e., by matter susceptible of slight motion or vibration; and let us represent the body by a vessel filled with water in which the tuning fork is partly immersed. Suppose now that the tuning fork is energized from without, or in other words that it receives an outward impulse which sets it in vibration. The tiny motion of the tuning fork will be transmitted to the water in which it is immersed, creating visible motion in the water. It is possible in this way to represent the origin of all action (motion of the body, i.e., the water) in passion (motion of the soul, i.e., the tuning fork) as analogous to the transmission and magnification of motion in and through matter exclusively.

Now let it be supposed that there are two such complexes of tuning fork and water vessel, and that the vibration of one tuning-fork induces a sympathetic vibration of the other. All of the essential conditions for the functioning of the sympathy mechanism are now present, and presumably the addition to the complex of sensoria, the conductors of motion from the outside world to the tuning-fork soul, would make it possible to carry the analogy as far as desired. Although it is not intended by this account to affirm positively that Smith's psychology requires the principle that the soul is material, it is intended to imply that the origination of all action in passion and the ubiquity of sympathy in Smith's sense are intelligible, and perhaps only intelligible, by the reduction of mind to

---

so delightful to himself that he almost forgets to enquire into the primary forces which set the action. He describes the mutual action and reaction of the passions with more fidelity than the passions themselves."

body. In other words, it is probable that one of Smith's unspoken premises is that the most essential phenomenon of human life is the induced motion of matter.[34]

Such an account of the mechanism of a material soul serves well enough to explain the responses of each man's sentiments to those of any other. Indeed it serves too well. Its very success is what forces us to ask, How, if each man's spirit responds passively to the stimuli of other men's behavior, can it so far insulate itself from those stimuli to judge of them – to approve or disapprove of them? There is an answer which seems to leave intact the mechanistic materiality of the soul: there are vibrations so minute that they produce no discernible effect upon a tuning fork exposed to them; and there are vibrations so intense that a tuning fork exposed to them will be unable to duplicate them in itself. But moral disapprobation does not mean the simple inability of the judge to reproduce the passions of the object of judgment. It means rather an unwillingness to do so. The judge renders judgment after he juxtaposes the passion of the object of judgment and the cause that excited that passion, and finds the two to be disproportionate, the one to the other. The second tuning fork does not simply react to the first; it deliberates the manner of its reaction, and reflects its moral judgment in the decision that it takes regarding the intensity of the reaction. In the largest number of cases, the judge will be estimating his reaction to occurrences to which the object of judgment was of course party, but to which the judge could not have been party. But this would not be possible for mere matter, which, as matter, cannot move itself, i.e., cannot, unstimulated, stimulate itself, or "imagine" itself party to a stimulus.

We are now confronted by this considerable difficulty: If all action originates in passion, soul must be reducible to body; soul and body are merged in matter, and action and passion are merged in motion. But we have seen how the possibility of moral judgment precludes the reduction of soul to

---

34 Cf. Hobbes, *Leviathan*, ch. 6 *passim*. See also Aristotle, *De Anima*, 405b32–407a2, but especially 406b24–26.

body. Smith, however, affirmed both the origin of action in passion and the possibility of moral judgment. Apart from the fact that Smith appears involved in an inconsistency, what meaning does the inconsistency itself have? I believe it means that the vindication of commercial society required Smith to speak of the passions of the body as the essence of man's humanity, or of human nature. But for reasons which we may, for convenience, refer to as the influence upon him of classical morality, he was unwilling to abandon the possibility of moral judgment. This is the first, and far from the least important instance of the tension between the natural and the moral that informs so much of Smith's doctrine. That crucial tension, to which we shall recur later, and a passing intimation of the stresses that play upon a materialistic theory are what we may regard as the lesson of this part of the discussion.

From the relation between sympathy and morality we know that general approbation of conduct is not to be regarded as the sign but as the origin of moral good or virtue, which is to say that whatever is "universally" approved is by definition right, or *becomes* right. We can scarcely avoid the crucial question, Is that which is approved, approved because it is virtuous, or is it rather virtuous because it is approved by "all?" Smith's formulation of the matter leads us to conclude that the virtuous is so by reason of the sympathy of the passions that generates approbation. In effect the criterion of human excellence develops from the passions which form the foundation of human nature as Smith conceived it. The moral order is regarded as derivative from and posterior to human nature rather than anterior to, or at least co-originate with it, although it would be reasonable to expect that the end of any purposeful process must be at least co-originate with, if not anterior to, the process itself. In this respect the teaching of Smith and of the modern authors whom he resembles differs profoundly from all teleological views of the whole, whether Christian or, pagan, by which the excellence of any species was conceived as leading rather than following the existence of that class of things, or as providing a norm towards which that species naturally tended. But we need hardly be surprised that Adam Smith thus takes his place in the train of the great modern philosophers who, in this or some other way, rejected the ancient principle of a substantive right by nature.

It might be thought that a criterion of moral right based upon "universal" approbation would come to ruin upon the obvious unlikelihood of any sentiment or conduct actually finding favor with every indifferent, impartial, or even reasonable man. But Smith does not, in the final analysis, require that the approbation be actually accorded for the act in question to be virtuous. What is necessary is that the act be deserving of the approbation or sympathy of every sane and disinterested spectator.[35] But if that approbation is not actually forthcoming, how is the virtue of a truly virtuous deed to be ascertained? Is a form of traditional natural right tacitly assumed? And further, how is the agent to govern himself and seek virtue if the outward means of recognizing it might be totally absent? Light will be cast on these problems if we examine the subject of virtue from the point of view of the agent, not, as we have hitherto done, from the point of view of the spectator.

Adam Smith's explicit doctrine is that each man will act virtuously when he wins the approbation of his conscience, of "the man within his breast" who is the vicar and symbol of all spectators.[36] Conscience is the final arbiter of morality, which means that formally the moral law is generated by each agent for his own guidance. It is generated by reference to the behest of a "man within" who speaks with the voice and in the name of all spectators or men without. "The spectator" is meaningful as the representative of all human beings outside the agent, and "all spectators" are coextensive with "all other men." And that the spectators are represented as having, for their decisive characteristics, nothing but impartiality and reason or sanity is a way of saying that virtue means to do what is consonant, not with the approbation of persons having extraordinary powers of moral judgment, but rather with the passions of other men as others, viz., simply as living human beings. To obey con-

---

35 *Theory of Moral Sentiments*, Pt. I, Sect. I, Ch. V, p. 24–5; Pt. II, Sect. I, Ch. II, p. 69.

36 Ibid., e.g., Pt. III, Ch. II, p. 130; Pt. III, Ch. III, p. 147.

science or to listen to the man within the breast is to act always within the limits imposed by the requirements of "all others" considered as human beings simply. The moral law derived from the behest of conscience so conceived, looking to the requirements of others as such or human beings as human simply rather than as somehow qualified, is based upon what we now call the equal rights of all men. Stated most generally, this conception of morality leads to the conclusion that virtue means acting with regard to the equal rights of all human beings as such, viz., as equal to each other. Clearly all human beings are formally equal to each other in respect of their common attribute of possessing life. No one has ever affirmed, and Adam Smith certainly did not affirm, the equality of all men in respect of desert, goodness, size, strength, or any other such attribute.[37]

Understanding by equality, then, equality in being human, i.e., in the right to life and to the pursuit of what supports life, Smith's very important reduction of human perfection to loving ourselves only as our neighbour is found capable of loving us[38] becomes intelligible as each man doing for himself as much as, but no more than, what is consistent with the self-preservation of others; or in other words, to exercise

---

37 It is true that Smith's famous figure of the philosopher and the porter (Wealth of Nations, Bk. I, Ch. II, pp. 28–9) seems to assert the substantial natural equality of all men in respect of intelligence. But we must observe that Smith's statement is full of qualifications, the bearing of which is given by the following fact: Smith wrote, "When [the philosopher and the porter] came into the world, and for the first six or eight years of their existence, they were, perhaps, very much alike," etc. Cannan, in his edition, notes that "'Perhaps' is omitted in eds. 2 and 3, and restored in the errata to ed. 4." Still, the import of the passage is in the direction of natural equality. We might add that Smith's argument is quite indecisive. Everyone will admit that education and habituation, or "division of labor," lead to large differences among people. But one proves nothing about equality by showing that if Socrates had had to grow his food and make his clothing, he would have been much more like a porter than he was.

38 Theory of Moral Sentiments, Pt. I, Sect. I, Ch. V, p. 25.

one's rights to the full within the limits imposed by the equal rights of all others as such is the right rule of life.[39] We now perceive one segment of the straight line that joins Adam Smith's moral philosophy with some of his most famous doctrines concerning society and polity; surely capitalism as the system of free competition, and liberal polity as the system of free conduct and democratic rule, are intelligible as practical embodiments of the principle of equal rights meant always to be exercised fully, but never a jot in excess.

When conscience is so seen in its intimate relation with sympathy, it becomes clear that conscience is, for Smith, the innate means by which every human being, as human, has direct, if imperfect, knowledge of the natural rights of "all others." Not only are all men essentially equal in the possession of natural human rights, but they are all essentially equal in possessing conscience, the psychic function by which those rights, and hence the morally right, become known. When nature is not conceived as embodying the substantive norm of right life, man must somehow evolve that norm from within himself. If the natural norm is simply a formal principle such as "the right life inheres in respecting the natural rights of others," the substance of that right and those rights must be accessible directly to each human being, or the possibility of right life must evanesce. It is "conscience" that makes the substance of the moral order intelligible to each human being as such. Indeed Smith writes, "What can be added to the happiness of the man who is in health, who is out of debt, and has a clear

---

39 This view is well illustrated by the following passage from the *Theory of Moral Sentiments*: "In the race for wealth, for honours, and preferments, [every man] may run as hard as he can, and strain every nerve and every muscle, in order to outstrip all his competitors. But if he should justle, or throw down any of them, the indulgence of the spectators is entirely at an end." Pt. II, Sect. II, Ch. II, p. 83. The bearing of this dictum upon the reasoning of the *Wealth of Nations* need hardly be pointed out. William Grampp implies, incorrectly, I believe, that Smith's teaching on natural rights emerges in the *Lectures* rather than in the *Theory of Moral Sentiments*. See Grampp, "Adam Smith and the Economic Man," *Journal of Political Economy*, vol. 56, p. 326.

conscience? . . . This situation, however, may very well be called the natural and ordinary state of mankind . . . this really is the state of the greater part of men."[40] The happiness of the greater part of mankind thus seems to be a direct outgrowth of their compliance with the moral law, betokened by their clear conscience.

One crucial aspect of excellence from the point of view of the agent remains to be considered: What is it that impels the agent to heed the inner voice of conscience? The question cannot be ignored, for the problem of morality is not simply coterminous with the problem of the "origin" of norms, nor yet with the problem of the means by which the norms come to be perceived by agents. The problem of morality includes the problem of the motivation of the agent, or what induces him to act consistently with his perception of the right. To this point in our study, Smith might be said to have described the legislative and judicial forces of conscience. Is there an executive power present, to correspond to the law-giving passions? It is to this question that we now turn.

Smith does not proceed in the order that we shall follow here, but the matter becomes clearer if we begin with his division of the virtues into two classes, the amiable and the respectable.[41] This distinction flows directly from the precept "that to feel much for others and little for ourselves, that to restrain our selfish, and to indulge our benevolent affections, constitutes the perfection of human nature."[42] As we have seen, excellence is derivative from sympathy between agent

40 *Theory of Moral Sentiments*, Pt. I, Sect. III, Ch. I, p. 45.

41 Ibid., Pt. I, Sect. I, Ch. V.

42 Ibid., Pt. I, Sect. I, Ch. V, p. 25. Also Pt. III, Ch. III, p. 152; "The man of the most perfect virtue, the man whom we naturally love and revere the most, is he who joins, to the most perfect command of his own original and selfish feelings, the most exquisite sensibility both to the original and sympathetic feeling of others. The man who, to all the soft, the amiable, and the gentle virtues, joins all the great, the awful, and the respectable, must surely be the natural and proper object of our highest love and admiration."

and spectator, which is to say that the doing of every virtuous deed implies the entire participation of the spectator in the manifest passion of the agent. The spectator must make an effort so to enter into the passion of a being outside himself. Indulgence of his benevolent affections is the form which that effort takes; and this is feeling much for others. The spectator can succeed in this only if the agent himself has first made the effort necessary so to modify his passion that its manifestation will be supportable by any other person.[43] That effort takes the form of a restraint of the selfish affections; and it results from feeling little for oneself, or not pursuing the selfish impulse to vent one's passions in their natural violence nor refusing the heavy effort of restraint. The perfect man will embody both the amiable virtues, which in effect are the virtues of spectators as such, and the respectable virtues, those belonging to agents as such. The perfect man will be the perfect spectator or judge, not in the sense of having the keenest and broadest powers of discernment but rather in having the greatest measure of sensibility to the pleasures and pains of all other human beings as such. The active[44] exercise of "spectatorial" virtue consists of passion, a sympathetic "feeling for" others, which is a natural consequence of that pity, love, or fellow-feeling that every human being has in some degree for every other human being alive.

The perfect man will also possess the virtues of the agent, or what we might term the active virtues, which are the excellences that evoke the approbation of spectators. The active virtues are practiced for the sake of that approbation or, with equal accuracy, to escape the contrary disapprobation. Above all "external" things the contempt or disregard of their fellows is intolerable to mankind;[45] and one component of their elemental self-love is what we may properly speak of as self-

---

43 E.g., Ibid., Pt. II, Sect. II, Ch. II, p. 83.

44 We say "active" with the understanding that, as has been pointed out above (page 14), all virtues, i.e., all virtuous "actions," are ultimately intelligible as passive or proceeding from passion.

45 E.g., *Theory of Moral Sentiments*, Pt. I, Sect. III, Ch. II, p. 61:

regard or self-respect. Smith refers to it as a regard for the requirements of one's dignity.[46] At its best it is what Smith regularly refers to as magnanimity. Like that impulse which is the motive of amiable virtue, magnanimous self-regard is a passion or emotion, a fact that Smith makes clear in those passages in which he establishes magnanimity as the distinguishing virtue of savage society.[47]

One outstanding inference from the foregoing is that the perfection of human nature consists in the play of two passions which, as passions, may be deemed the natural inheritance of every human being.[48] We need not question the extent to which each individual does in fact embody these passions, and in what way; surely men are by nature unequal in their sensibility or "passivity."[49] It suffices for our immediate purpose (which, it will be remembered, was to examine the "executive" meaning of the presence of conscience in the human breast) to realize that the impulsive force which men obey when they heed the voice of the inner man, is sentiment or passion. Appropriately, not only the legislative and judicial, but also the executive branch of the agent spirit is passional.

The reduction of the inner impulsion towards excellence to the play of a pair of elemental passions is of importance to

---

"Compared with the contempt of mankind, all other external evils are easily supported."

46 E.g., Ibid., Pt. III, Ch. III, pp. 147, 148; Pt. IV, Ch. II, p. 191.

47 Ibid., Pt. V, Ch. II, pp. 206–7.

48 Cf. Xenophon, *Memorabilia*, II, vi, 21–2: "Ah, Critobulus, but there is a strange complication in these matters. Some elements in man's nature make for friendship: men need one another, feel pity, work together for their common good, and, conscious of the facts, are grateful to one another. But there are hostile elements in men. For holding the same things to be honourable and pleasant, they fight for them, fall out and take sides. Strife and anger lead to hostility, covetousness to enmity, jealousy to hatred. Nevertheless, through all these barriers friendship slips, and unites the gentle natures." (*Loeb Classical Library* ed., p. 137.)

49 *Theory of Moral Sentiments*, Pt. I, Sect. I, Ch. IV, p. 19; Pt. III, Ch. III, p. 152.

Smith's teaching in a variety of ways. In the first place, the traditional idea of moral education through exhortation is inferentially rejected. The true provenience of virtue is seen as the indefeasible passions themselves, not the careful conquest of the passions. This position accords perfectly with Smith's general doctrine of the inefficacy of exhortation in producing virtue, and the larger impotence of the reason to rule the passions.[50] Substituted for the classic conception of a "second nature" produced by habituation to virtuous conduct and to the desire for excellence, is the conception of a passionately stimulated adherence to rules of proper behavior. The devotion is to the rule as such and not to the excellence as such.[51] This may be made clear by contrasting the state of mind of the virtuous man whose excellence is supposed to proceed from traditional hortatory moral education with that of the man whose excellence flows from his veneration of a rule. The former develops an habitual disposition to do the right thing, by force of which he derives satisfaction from doing right and is pained by the necessity or the prospect of doing ill. Another way of saying this would be that he has the habitual disposition, not only to do Justice in general, or to be Liberal, Temperate, and Courageous, but equally to do this particular act of justice and to act in this particular situation with liberality or temperance. The latter sort of individual, although he has a disposition to do right, has triumphed over his refractory passions only in that he prefers Justice to Injustice and Temperance to Intemperance; yet doing the just or temperate action will nonetheless generate pain and conflict within him. Thus Smith says of such a man, "Though his heart therefore is

50 Ibid., Pt. I, Sect. I, Ch. I, p. 12.

51 Ibid., Pt. III, Ch. V, p. 142: "The motive of his actions may be no other than a reverence for the established rule of duty . . . ." James Bonar, in *Moral Sense*, p. 222, affirms Smith's view to be that "man is not the slave of the passions." But man is emancipated from his passions only in the measure to which he is enslaved by a rule.

not warmed with any grateful affection, he will strive to act as if it was."[52] In effect the passions are conquered but never governed. The habit which the virtuous man acquires is the habit of consulting the rule, not the habit of right conduct which would make the rule as such superfluous; and since there is *no* man who can rise above this pitch of excellence, or "without this sacred regard to general rules, there is no man whose conduct can be much depended upon,"[53] it seems to follow that excellence inevitably remains outside of human nature proper and must exist as an uneasy balance of opposed forces, the passions, that are at the core of nature.

As has been suggested above, there is a connection between Smith's conception of the place of reason in the whole order of being, and man's moral, and therefore political, possibilities. According to Smith, philosophy, man's rational enterprise, leads to many conclusions which by their very rationality conflict with the order of nature. It does so in the sphere of morality by seeking ends which man's nature will not permit of. Moral philosophy in the past at any rate guided itself by those conditions of man which it perceived to be the best. But nature has forged certain links of cause and effect against which the efforts of philosophy and reason must remain powerless. Those links, in truth, *are* nature, and as we have seen immediately above the causes are the indefeasible passions, and the effects are human conduct as it is and as it must inevitably be. We cannot forget Smith's claim that the *Theory of Moral Sentiments* "is not concerning a matter of right. . . but concerning a matter of fact. We are not at present examining upon what principles a perfect being would approve of the punishment of bad actions; but upon what principles so weak and imperfect a creature as man actually and in fact approves of it."[54]

The meaning and bearing of moral philosophy itself must be reconsidered in the light of the disappearance of moral edu-

---

52   *Theory of Moral Sentiments*, Pt. III, Ch. V, p. 162.

53   Ibid., Pt. III, Ch. V, p. 163.

54   Ibid., Pt. II, Sect. I, Ch. V, p. 77n.

cation as exhortation and habituation in right ways. Smith wrote

> If it was possible, by precept and exhortation, to inspire the mind with fortitude and magnanimity, the ancient systems of propriety would seem sufficient to do this. Or if it was possible, by the same means, to soften it into humanity, and to awaken the affections of kindness and general love towards those we live with, some of the pictures which the benevolent system [of moral philosophy] presents us, might seem capable of producing this effect.[55]

Yet he continues to affirm the fundamentally "practical" character of moral philosophy, or its intelligibility as a means to make people "good."[56] The way in which the end is to be gained is indicated by the proposition, "The great secret of education is to direct vanity to proper objects."[57] Moral philosophy is still to work upon men to seek good and avoid evil, but their passionate self regard will be employed as the means. It goes without saying that the good must itself be understood as having a nature that makes it attainable by such means. Smith's outlook upon moral philosophy accounts for what we might call the "psychological" tone of this moral work. In a sense, the first purpose of the book is to describe the motions of the soul – its passions and its actions – which are the sources of morality and of moral standards. Upon the premise that the standards of right proceed from a motion of the human soul, viz., "sympathy," moral philosophy truly cannot escape being drawn into the orbit of "psychology" or description of the ways and motives of most men. Smith significantly contrasted his own conception of moral philosophy with that of earlier writers, and his appreciation of the gulf between the centuries

---

55 Ibid., Pt. VII, Sect. II, Ch. IV, p. 307.

56 Ibid., Pt. VII, Sect. II, Ch. I, p. 293: "To direct the judgments of this inmate [of the breast] is the great purpose of all systems of morality."

57 Ibid., Pt. VI, Sect. III, p. 259.

is perhaps best vindicated by a fact relating to the moral writings of Aristotle himself. Aristotle composed a treatise on the ways and motives of men, descriptive of the passions and actions of their souls as these relate to moral things; but the work is entitled the *Rhetoric*, not the *Ethics*. The essentially descriptive nature of the *science* pertaining to the art or technique of rhetoric is indicated by Aristotle's remark to the effect that the function of rhetoric "is not so much to persuade, as to find out in each case the existing means of persuasion."[58] *Rhetoric* is indeed an art or technique, a means for working upon men, not to make them "good" but to make them manageable; which suggests a reason for the interest shown in the *Rhetoric* by such a pioneer of modern philosophy as Thomas Hobbes. That treatise has an instant appeal to all those who prefer realistic moral philosophy when realistic is taken as meaning "not concerning matters of right but matters of fact." Perhaps it would not be improper to speak of the *Theory of Moral Sentiments* as an example of the rhetoricization of moral philosophy in recent centuries, for all of the reasons touched upon above.

In the next place, the reduction of human motives to two elemental passions, and of human excellence to the resultant of those passions, dispenses with the requirement that the utility of social virtue or, more generally, of society itself, be rationally perceived by men. The doctrine that the desirability of virtue does not depend upon any calculation of the utility of virtue to preservation, is the burden of Part IV of the *Theory of Moral Sentiments*. The principle has far-reaching implications. Social virtue is for the sake of society, and society is for the sake of preservation of life. Society, and hence the most potent instrument for man's preservation, does not flow from rational decisions to procure a useful end, but rather from the passions directly.[59] In general, the means for safeguarding preservation have been seen to evolve from the free motion of

---

58   Aristotle, *Rhetoric*, 1355b. (Loeb ed)

59   Cf. *Theory of Moral Sentiments*, Pt. VI, Sect III, p. 259.

the passions.[60] The separation from reason of both social virtue and social arrangements or polity (as instruments of utility to life) and their attribution to passion instead, led Smith to the resounding conclusion that the best for society follows from actions traceable not to reason but to passion. It is not a coincidence that this very Part of the *Theory of Moral Sentiments* announces the famous figure of the invisible hand:

> [The rich] are led by an invisible hand to make nearly the same distribution of the necessaries of life, which would have been made, had the earth been divided into equal portions among all its inhabitants, and thus without intending it, without knowing it, advance the interest of the society, and afford means to the multiplication of the species.[61]

The doctrine of the invisible hand has occasionally been interpreted to signify the intervention of Divine Providence in human affairs, the invisible hand the hand of God, and the rule of the invisible hand the sovereignty of Natural Law or the law of God. This is intelligible only in so far as the behest of God is conceived as identical with the behest of passion.

The singular prepotence of passion over reason has an important bearing upon the venerable problem of the compatibility of philosophy and society. In so far as society is itself the object of philosophic inquiry, society can be radically endangered by philosophy, whence arises the issue of compatibility. Smith's position on the relation of passion and reason suggests his position on the compatibility of society and philosophy. Man's passion teaches him to seek the preservation of his life and to avoid death. The dread of death is "one of the most important principles in human nature . . . the great poison to the happiness, but the great restraint upon the injustice of mankind, which, while it afflicts and mortifies the individual, guards and protects the society."[62] Needless to say, the social utility of fear of death proceeds from the indefeasibility of that

---

60   Above, p. 5. In this, Smith is closer to Rousseau than to Hobbes.

61   *Theory of Moral Sentiments*, Pt. IV, Ch. I, p. 184–5.

62   Ibid., Pt. I, Sect. I, Ch. I, p. 13.

fear. The fear of death is no less than the sovereign weapon of society. Could it be conquered, its conqueror might become the mortal enemy of society, generally exempt from the social bond. It is important, therefore, that Smith believed the impotence of philosophy or reason to extend to its inability to free man from the fear of death.[63] Thus there can be no attack by philosophy upon society which society cannot repulse. It is a matter of history, however, that the passions of religious fervor differ from the promptings of reason and philosophy in this respect; and it would accordingly seem that the greater danger to the existence of society comes not from conviction bred of reason, which may be subverted by the fear of death, but from the passions born of religious fervor, which are not merely impervious to the fear of death but even seek the earthly termination for the sake of the martyr's crown beyond. The importance of this view of the matter will become clearer through the remaining portions of this essay, wherein will be discussed Smith's proposal to rely upon philosophy and science for the very defense of society against the power of otherworldly influence.

Another profoundly important inference from Smith's teaching on morality relates to the content of morality itself. The perfection of human nature was described as feeling much for others and little for ourselves, restraining our selfish and indulging our benevolent affections, and loving ourselves only as our neighbor is found capable of loving us. Smith juxtaposes the Christian law "to love our neighbour as we love ourselves" and the precept of nature "to love ourselves only as we love our neighbour, or what comes to the same thing, as our neighbour is found capable of loving us."[64] The one has always been understood to prescribe the measure of devotion owed to one's neighbor, the other clearly delimits the measure of devotion to oneself. The one is an exhortation to active benevolence, charity, and sacrifice; the other simply seeks the

---

63   "Fear and anxiety, . . . from which, reason and philosophy . . . in vain, attempt defend . . . man." Ibid., Pt. I, Sect. I, Ch. I, p. 12.

64   *Theory of Moral Sentiments*, Pt. I, Sect. I, Ch. V, p. 25.

limits of good which a man may properly do himself.[65] It is clear that these two dicta are not identical; also that they do not necessarily conflict. Smith does not himself raise the question of the relation between them. Yet we cannot avoid noticing that, in a later passage of the *Theory of Moral Sentiments*, Smith begins his discussion of the order in which individuals are recommended to our care and attention, by adopting the Stoic principle: "Every man . . . is first and principally recommended to his own care."[66] "After himself, the members of his own family, those who usually live in the same house with him, his parents, his children, his brothers and sisters, are naturally the objects of his warmest affections."[67] Smith's lengthy and detailed account in Part IV of the *Theory of Moral Sentiments* identifies the natural with the Stoic, not with the Christian precept. If it is natural for man to love himself best, it is naturally impossible for him to love even the members of his immediate family, much less his neighbor, as he loves himself.

When we noticed earlier[68] the orientation of Smith's doctrine upon rights rather than upon duties, and when we observed the crucial importance to this formulation of the idea of others as such, we prepared the way for the present conclusion that one of the critical problems of morality and of moral philosophy, from Smith's point of view, is the definition of rights from the vantage of others; or the identification of what things are owed to others in virtue of their human character simply. This orientation of morality is signalized by the organization of Part VI of the *Theory of Moral Sentiments*, which is entitled "Of the Character of Virtue." It is divided into three sections, of which the third, "Of Self-Command," deals with the purely formal excellence of self-control in all directions. The first two sections, however, defining the real content of virtue, are: I. "Of the Character of the Individual, so far as it

---

65   Ibid., Pt. I, Sect. I, Ch. V, p. 25.

66   Ibid., Pt. VI, Sect. II, Ch. I, p. 219.

67   *Ibid.*

68   Above, pp. 21 ff.

affects his own Happiness; or of Prudence;" and II. "Of the Character of the Individual, so far as it can affect the Happiness of Other People." Morality and therefore moral science exist upon the tension between what the individual may do in his own interest and what he must concede to the interest, or rights, of others as such. In this, as in many fundamental respects, Smith is intelligible as the disciple of Hobbes, the translator of Hobbeanism into an order of society. It can be said that Adam Smith's broad view of the present matter, expressed by him with elegant and laborious diffusion, is compressed by Hobbes into the single paragraph in *Leviathan* wherein complaisance is declared to be the fifth law of nature. Hobbes wrote of complaisance that it requires "that every man strive to accommodate himself to the rest," and vindicated it by the proposition that "every man, not only by right, but also by necessity of nature, is supposed to endeavour all he can, to obtain that which is necessary for his conservation; [therefore] he that shall oppose himself against it, for things superfluous, is guilty of the war that thereupon is to follow . . ."[69]

Smith's view of the pre-eminence in morality of rights as opposed to duties is illustrated clearly by the manner in which he divides the science of morality into parts. Moral philosophy had been treated by his predecessors in a number of characteristic ways, he thought: By the ancients it had been handled throughout in a vague style that bespoke the enduring difficulty of reducing the principles of conduct to strict precision. By the "casuists," i.e., the Catholic and Protestant theologians who discussed moral questions in terms of "casus conscientiae," (problems of conscience), moral philosophy was treated as if all of human conduct could be reduced to precise formulas and rules. Smith affirms that, in truth, moral philosophy is composed of two parts, namely, Ethics, the domain of all the virtues save justice, and Jurisprudence, the science of justice. Casuistry must be rejected entirely, on the principle that it vainly seeks to prescribe the duties of the good man, which is not a fit subject for science since those duties depend upon cir-

---

69   Hobbes, *Leviathan*, Ch. 15, pp. 138–9.

cumstances which not only cannot be known in advance but can scarcely be "known" at all, for they are present only to the passions and are resolved by the passions.[70] Ethics, concerned with matters arbitrated by the sentiments, is the part of moral philosophy in which precision is not to be looked for. Jurisprudence, as the part of moral philosophy treating of justice, will expound the rules to be administered by judges, which rules will correspond to the exact rights of the members of society against each other. Jurisprudence, the science of justice, becomes at once *the* science of political existence par excellence and the science of what each may, by force if necessary, require of his fellows. Hence "the principles upon which [the rules of justice] either are, or ought to be founded, are the subject of a particular science, of all sciences by far the most important, but hitherto, perhaps, the least cultivated, that of natural jurisprudence."[71] The science of polity is the science of rights. In the adoption of the science of justice (justice understood as that minimal virtue requiring respect of others' rights) as the science of polity, and the rejection of casuistry, Smith affirms the legitimacy of justice and rights, and the impossibility of benevolence and duty as the principles of social life.

Smith's teaching concerning justice is the obverse of his doctrine respecting benevolence, and the two must be studied together. Justice as the political virtue par excellence is reduced by Smith to contractual reciprocity, the principle which relates singularly to those associations of men which exist for the sake of exchange, inferentially including in that category the political association. It reflects the passion that causes men to render to others, not their desert according to merit, for example, but what they can claim as living human beings impelled and licensed by nature to seek their preserva-

---

70 "It may be said in general of the works of the casuists that they attempted, to no purpose, to direct by precise rules what it belongs to feeling and sentiment only to judge of." *Theory of Moral Sentiments*, Pt. VII, Sect. IV, p. 339.

71 *Theory of Moral Sentiments*, Pt. VI, Sect. II, Introd., p. 218.

tion as the end.[72] Hence injustice relates to injuries by which a
man is deprived of such things, and in such a way that he is
properly provoked to resentment. Resentment is properly provoked *only* by injustice;[73] and proper resentment alone justifies
retaliation or the use of force. Hence "retaliation seems to be
the great law which is dictated to us by Nature"[74] and is the
force that guarantees justice; and thus it is that the just comes
to mean hurting those who hurt us.[75] Justice is literally the
enforceable virtue[76] because only the defense of the means of
life can justify force or (retaliatory) attack on life.[77]

Related to this explanation of the "enforceability" of justice is Smith's position on the uniqueness of justice as the sole
virtue whose requirements are intelligible precisely and in

---

72 Cf. Hobbes, *Leviathan*, Ch. 15 (Molesworth, p. 137): "Justice of
actions, is by writers divided into *commutative*, and *distributive*:
and the former they say consisteth in proportion arithmetical;
the latter in proportion geometrical. Commutative therefore,
they place in the equality of value of the things contracted for;
and distributive, in the distribution of equal benefit, to men of
equal things contracted for; and distributive, in the distribution
of equal benefit, to men of equal merit. As if it were injustice to
sell dearer than we buy; or to give more to a man than he merits.
The value of all things contracted for, is measured by the appetite
of the contractors; and therefore the just value, is that which they
be contented to give. And merit, besides that which is by
covenant, where the performance on one part, meriteth the performance of the other part, and falls under justice commutative,
not distributive, is not due by justice; but is rewarded of grace
only."

Also, Ibid., p. 141: the ninth law of nature the breach of
which is pride, is "that every man acknowledge another for his
equal by nature for the sake of every man's right to pursue his
preservation."

73 *Theory of Moral Sentiments*, Pt. II, Sect. II, Ch. I, p. 79.

74 Ibid., Pt. II, Sect. II, Ch. I, p. 82.

75 Ibid., Pt. VI, Sect. II, Introd., p. 218.

76 Ibid., Pt. II, Sect. II, Ch. I, pp. 79–80.

77 Ibid., Pt. II, Sect. I, Ch. II, p. 71; Pt. II, Sect. II, Ch. I, pp. 80–1.

advance, so far as to be entirely reducible to rules. The general implication of this is that it is easy to comply with the requirements of justice because it is easy to know them. Another view was taken in ancient times, when it was thought that, although to know one should be just is not difficult, to know what precisely to do at the call of justice is extremely difficult.[78] We may relate the two principles here spoken of by saying that justice would not be the virtue completely reducible to rules if it had not first been defined as the virtue relating entirely to reciprocity. Thus if justice were permitted to include any element of what was previously known as equity, or of mutability, or if it related to the balance among the parts of the soul, it would not inherit the peculiar dignity with which Smith endows it, nor would it be merely *the* political virtue.[79] It should be noted, also, that in so reasoning on justice, Smith furthers his abiding enterprise of removing the social life of man from a dependence upon rational realization of utility to a purely passional basis. Thus justice is guaranteed not by any rational perception of the good of society which is produced by the punishment of injustice, but rather by the passion of retaliation, one of a number of supremely important socially useful passions, infinitely more reliable than reason.[80]

Benevolence, like justice, proceeding from the passions of the mind that seek the good of others, is explicitly rejected as a principle of political association, not only theoretically, as in the *Theory of Moral Sentiments,* but also in the practical way of excluding it from the system propounded in the *Wealth Of*

---

78 Ibid., Pt. III, Ch. VI, p. 175–6; Pt. VII, Sect. IV, p. 327; *Nicomachean Ethics*, 1137a 8–15.

79 Cf. Montesquieu, *Spirit of Laws*, XX, ii: "The commercial spirit produces in men a certain sentiment of exact justice which is opposed on the one hand to brigandage, and on the other to those moral virtues which lead one not always to discuss his own interests with rigidity, and which allow him to subordinate them to those of others."

80 *Theory of Moral Sentiments*, Pt. II, Sect. I, Ch. V, p. 77n.

Nations.[81] Smith compares justice to the pillar, and benevolence to the ornament of political life as such,[82] on the ground that justice guarantees to each man his rights in the means of life and preservation, whereas benevolence procures to him those things in which he has no right by the high rule of *quid pro quo* or life-giving reciprocity. That *the* political virtue should be the one which flows directly from the requirements of self-preservation is a point of some importance, for it suggests the principle upon which polity itself is based: polity or society is for the sake of the preservation of life, rather than, as was once supposed, for the sake of the perfection of life.[83]

Man is by nature social, but only because nature itself means the preservation of life. We have observed Smith to say, "Self-preservation, and the propagation of the species, are the great ends which Nature seems to have proposed in the formation of all animals;"[84] and to this we must now add, ". . . the immense fabric of human society, that fabric which to raise and support seems in this world, if I may say so, to have been the peculiar and darling care of Nature. . . ."[85] The two ideas together form the conclusion that the end of nature is simulta-

---

81 Thus, we do not appeal to the benevolence of the butcher and baker, but to their self-interest and advantage to gain the ends of society. *Wealth of Nations*, Bk. I, Ch. II, p. 14.

82 *Theory of Moral Sentiments*, Pt. II, Sect. II, Ch. III, pp. 85-6.

83 Cf. Hobbes, *Leviathan*, Ch. 17 (Molesworth, III, p. 158): " . . . the commonwealth, which, to define it, is one person, of whose acts a great multitude, by mutual covenants one with another, have made themselves every one the author, to the end he may use the strength and means of them all, as he shall think expedient, for their peace and common defence."

With this, contrast Aristotle, *Politics*, Ch. 9, Bk. III; but especially 1280a32 et seq.: "But a state exists for the sake of a good life, and not for the sake of life only: if life only were the object, slaves and brute animals might form a state, but they cannot, for they have no share in happiness or in a life of free choice."

84 *Theory of Moral Sentiments*, Pt. II, Sect. I, Ch. V, p. 77n.

85 Ibid., Pt. II, Sect. II, Ch. III, p. 86.

neously the preservation of life and the support of society, the two made one by the proposition that man can subsist only in society.[86]

The exclusion of benevolence as the principle of society is related to Smith's conception of the end of political life and the principles of political association, as well as of human nature. Benevolence is practically impossible as the basis of life because it is in perpetual conflict with man's "needs" and hence with his deepest passions favoring self-preservation.

> Benevolence may, perhaps, be the sole principle of action in the Deity, and there are several not improbable arguments which tend to persuade us that it is so. It is not easy to conceive what other motive an independent and all-perfect Being, who stands in need of nothing external, and whose happiness is complete in himself, can act from. But whatever may be the case with the Deity, so imperfect a creature as man, the support of whose existence requires so many things external to him, must often act from many other motives.[87]

Most briefly stated, man cannot regularly afford the luxury of benevolence, and cannot *reasonably* submit to the regime that could overcome his passionate resistance to it as a sovereign social principle. Yet if we look into history, we see that it demonstrates the practical possibility of importing at least a large measure of benevolence and charity into the order of society. Europe generally, and England in particular knew an order of social life oriented upon norms of benevolence perhaps as late as the years of Henry VIII.[88] As a point of fact, it might be objected to this statement that, far from being an age of benevolence and charity, those remote centuries were a period of malevolence and gross cruelty, as the penal institutions, especially the visitation of heavy punishment upon

---

86   Ibid., Pt. II, Sect. II, Ch. III, p. 85.

87   Ibid., Pt. VII, Sect. II, Ch. III, p. 305.

88   See for example the *History of England* by J. A. Froude, vol. 1, ch. I.

chronic vagabonds and heretics, seem to suggest. But if the matter be considered, it will appear that precisely where the rule is charity, the safeguards against malingering and shiftlessness must be the most efficient; and where the cornerstone of all of life is faith, few offenses can appear more grave than miscreancy. In truth, the early age conceived itself as living by the rule of Christianity. That rule included the precept "that if any would not work, neither should he eat," in conjunction with "be not weary in well doing."[89] The age was in this respect as much or as little cruel as the doctrine of St. Paul. It is of course true that medieval society was benevolent, in Smith's sense of the term, in inverse proportion to the importance of commerce therein; and commerce was surely present in Christian society. Yet Christian society was not commercial society, and if not benevolence or unrequited giving, then at least "the common good" and not "gain" was the social norm endlessly preached to the people and at least nominally aimed at by their regimes. In this respect the difference between Catholic and Protestant teaching was not of great weight. Before public diversity of opinion generated the tolerance that embraces skepticism, all divinity, Protestant and Catholic alike, agreed in suppressing avarice however recognized, and in enjoining benevolence however understood.[90] We should make clear that we are not using benevolence in the wide sense in which it would have included mutual lenity between zealous Catholics and Protestants, but only in its Smithian sense denoting the provision of goods and services without *quid pro quo*.

But Smith rejected what his great antecessor called the fear of power invisible (i.e., loosely, ecclesiastical authority) as an element of political life.[91] We may avoid the troublesome subject of Smith's own fidelity as a believer, and pass directly to his pronouncement upon religion as the guarantor of benevo-

---

89   II Thess., iii, 10: 13.

90   Cf. Thomas Wilson's "A Discourse upon Usurie" (1572), reprinted with R. H. Tawney's introduction.

91   Cf. *Theory of Moral Sentiments*, Pt. III, Ch. V, p. 164: "the terrors of religion."

lence. He affirmed that religious morality must correspond to one of a pair of alternatives which make virtue consist either in obedience out of regard to God's reward and punishment, or in an abstract "fitness" attaching to the compliance of a subordinate with the will of a superior being. The first alternative identifies religious morality with "prudence," or concentration upon reward and punishment; the second with "propriety."[92] Smith explicitly rejected systems of morality which derive virtue from prudential considerations or considerations of utility,[93] and further rejected them implicitly by basing his own teaching upon propriety, the alternative principle to prudence. Yet his category of "prudential" clearly includes every system of religious morality that has actually governed in the western world. The Christian polity of benevolence at the behest of a dreaded power in heaven is thus rejected as a political solution.[94]

As we have seen, the impotence of moral education against the passions renders impossible the virtuous disposi-

---

92 Ibid., Pt. VII, Sect. II, Ch. III, p. 305.

93 See above p. 30.

94 To speculate on the reason for Smith's rejection of the fear of power invisible as a principle of social life is a great temptation. One of the rare passages in Smith's writings that bear upon the matter is to be found at the end of Ch. III, Sect. II, Pt. II of the *Theory of Moral Sentiments*: "The justice of God, however, we think, still requires, that he should hereafter avenge the injuries of the widow and the fatherless, who are here so often insulted with impunity. In every religion, and in every superstition that the world has ever beheld, accordingly, there has been a Tartarus as well as an Elysium; a place provided for the punishment of the wicked, as well as one for the reward of the just."

Cf. also Ibid., Pt. II, Sect. I, Ch. I, p. 81, where of the dead it is said that they are capable of feeling no human sentiment, seemingly disposing at once of pleasure and pain and reward and punishment in another world. Also Ibid., Pt. VI, Sect. III, p. 239: death is viewed with superstitious horror by the weak and inexperienced. With this compare John Rae, *Life of Adam Smith*, pp. 299–314 (London and New York, 1895).

tion that would provide the necessary guarantees of benevolence from within.

Besides the sanctions of ecclesiastical authority, there exists another means for procuring virtue among the members of society. That other instrumentality, treated by Adam Smith, is irresistible power in the prince or civil magistrate. We may say that Smith rejects fear of the prince as the principle of virtuous society because "to push [the magistrate's power over conduct] too far is destructive of all liberty, security, and justice."[95] This doctrine in the abstract is self-evident almost to being uninteresting, but as applied to the problem of virtuous or benevolent society, it is not without importance. Seemingly, the quest for "virtuous" society must be abandoned if to procure it the community is bound to submit to unreason or tyranny. Instead of seeking to procure virtue through civil or ecclesiastical coercion, the view seems to emerge that good society proceeds from maximum citizen "reason."[96] Justice, the *sine qua non* of society, is actually derivative from liberty rather than from inhibition; for justice is the product of free contract, and freedom means the freedom to do unlimited business. Apparently, freedom is to be understood as emancipation from those internal and external inhibitions upon conduct which are necessary to overcome the irrepressible passions. This leads to the Smithian conclusion that those things which the magistrate would be obliged to do if he were to administer the virtuous society would comprise the substance of tyranny. Paradoxically, the tyrant now appears as the magistrate who rules, not outside the law and for his own sake, but rigidly through the law and for the sake of admitted excellence.

---

95 *Theory of Moral Sentiments*, Pt. II, Sect. II, Ch. I, p. 81.

96 Perhaps there will be a question as to the consistency of this remark with foregoing assertions of Smith's belief in the subordination of reason in the largest sense. The rationality here intended is simply freedom from induced misconception, or superstition. Citizen rationality, as distinguished from human rationality simply, means indoctrination to non-irrational opinions.

We shall have occasion to refer at length to the free, secular, enlightened order of society that is the practical inference from these theoretical conceptions of Adam Smith.

* * *

There is another vantage from which Smith's moral orientation may profitably be examined, and that is the one that holds in view his teaching upon the four cardinal virtues – a teaching upon which, in one sense, his entire moral theory rests. According to Smith, prudence, justice, benevolence, and self-command are the excellences of the perfectly virtuous man, prudence being virtue in providing for one's happiness (scil. "needs"), benevolence and justice the virtues of the passions seeking the happiness of others, and self-command being the virtue which makes all other excellences possible, and is therefore itself the greatest of all virtues.[97] The immediate interest to us of this classification is in the fact that one of the four cardinal virtues of man, namely benevolence, has been wholly excluded from political life as such and in particular from the polity which is singularly associated with Smith's name. The large question into which we must now enter is, upon what principle can the exclusion of a cardinal virtue from polity be maintained?

We must take our bearings again by the broadest principles of Smith's teaching, the meaning of nature and the ends of political life. Nature means the force that seeks the perpetuation of vital motion in all things, and society is the device that nature has appointed to effect man's preservation in life. The exclusion from polity of one of the chief virtues is intelligible on the premise that there is an irreducible conflict between the requirements of that virtue and the requirements of the preservation of life. Indeed we have seen the evidence of Smith's belief in such a conflict when we noticed his assertion that benevolence could be the prevailing excellence only among beings like the Deity, literally perfect (i.e., complete), needing nothing. Man's needs govern, as they cause, his social exis-

---

97 *Theory of Moral Sentiments*, Pt. VI, passim.

tence; and his social existence is guaranteed by nature for his preservation. But preservation, needs, and nature, culminating in political society, conflict with an important excellence of man, leading us to the inference that there exists a tension not only between virtue and society but also between virtue and nature.[98]

The theme of the moral irresponsibility of nature, or of the failure of the natural and the noble to coincide in principle, is touched upon in Chapter 5, Part III of the *Theory of Moral Sentiments*. Following old traditions, Smith affirms that each virtue has its peculiar natural reward, industry, prudence and circumspection being crowned with success in every sort of business (i.e., with wealth and honor); and truth, justice and humanity earning the confidence, esteem and love of one's fellowmen. Paradoxically, however, man is moved by nature itself to be dissatisfied with this natural disposition, and to desire instead that the excellences that most strongly compel his love should be rewarded with every sort of desirable thing: "Man is by Nature directed to correct, in some measure, that distribution of things which she herself would otherwise have made. The rules which for this purpose she prompts him to follow, are different from those which she herself observes."[99] Speaking so, Smith draws a distinction between the simply natural and the human natural moral ways: man would not dispose as nature disposes.

But Smith goes beyond merely distinguishing between the moral ways of man and nature. He suggests that there is a difference in the quality or level of those ways. Man's inclination points to a "correction" of the simply natural. Characterizing man in his strife against the natural, Smith likens him to the

---

98 Cf. G. R. Morrow's remark on a similar strain in Hutcheson: "Hutcheson . . . [distinguished] between moral and natural good, i.e., between sentiments of moral approval and sensations of pleasure or pain. Natural good is connected with the pleasure of sense perception, moral good with the love or approval of disinterested observers." Morrow, "Significance of the Doctrine of Sympathy", p. 63.

99 *Theory of Moral Sentiments*, Pt. III, Ch. V, p. 168.

gods of the poets, "perpetually interposing, by extraordinary means, in favour of virtue, and in opposition to vice."[100] Man strives against nature in favor of virtue and in opposition to that efficient vice that succeeds in a natural world. Man reveals his partiality to virtue, and his moral superiority to nature, when he creates a hierarchy of the virtues, discriminating the more and the less meritorious ones and of course preferring, in a certain way, the more. Nature acknowledges no such hierarchy, but provides only that to each excellence there correspond some reward; or more exactly, that to each mode of behavior there be appended some determinate consequence for the agent.

Smith allows that the human viewpoint is sentimental – the virtues "may seem to possess [different degrees of merit and demerit] in the sentiments and passions of man"[101] – but indeed, it is not only man's discrimination of the lesser from the greater virtues, but also his discrimination of the virtuous from the vicious, as we saw earlier, that is informed by his passions. A sentimental origin is not, as sentimental, invalidating; it would seem that man's claim of moral superiority is a tenable one. There is, however, one apparent bar to it: natural in their origins are man's very dissensions from the natural moral disposition. If man's noble reservations against nature are themselves natural in their origin, then man's superiority to nature cannot be affirmed without qualifications. We are obliged to inquire into the mode and meaning of man's rejection of the natural moral disposition.

Man's rejection of the natural moral disposition is a rejection in wish or speech, not in action. Man wishes that certain virtues, which he admires greatly, would be rewarded differently, "better," than nature rewards them; but the virtues that man as man prefers are not the virtues that man as man acquires. He does not, in general, choose to act so as to deserve the most valuable rewards according to the rule of his own disposition; rather, he seems generally to act so as to deserve the most valuable rewards according to the rule of the natural

100 Ibid.
101 Ibid.

disposition. Smith affirms that man understands by "bettering his condition" gaining in wealth and place. In his practice, man indicates that he ranks the rewards in one way but the virtues to which those rewards correspond he ranks differently. That is to say, man's wishes accord with the human moral order but his practice accords with the natural moral order: in practice he seeks out those rewards which conduce to the favorite ends of nature – the preservation of life – and he must seek those ends in nature's way, by the practice of virtues that, as man, he rejects as ignoble.

Thus there is a sense in which man may be said to achieve moral superiority over nature: in wish, or speech alone, he rejects and rises above nature. And the fact that his reservations against the natural order are naturally inspired means that it is human nature to reject the simply natural. But what, in turn, is the meaning of the idea that it is nature which impels man to see by a light which is somehow his and not hers? The answer seems to be this: that when nature is conceived as void of moral norms, but rather only as what singularly relates actions and their consequences ("causes and effects"), those norms to which men will inevitably resort will not appear as natural yet cannot be conceded to be purely arbitrary without losing their worth as norms: the arbiter is in its essence the non-arbitrary. Smith's solution implies the simultaneous naturalness and arbitrariness of the normative ranking of the virtues: man is naturally disposed to reverse the natural. Then human nature is in some sense *sui generis*, not wholly an aspect of nature simply but partly a denial or negation of it. This is the dubious position Smith occupies in order to maintain the distinction between the ignoble while at the same time conceding the indifference of nature to nobility.

In the most general terms we might say that, when self-preservation is taken to be the ultimate goal or overriding end of nature, the end dictated by nature ceases to be identical with the good life in the full sense, or with virtue; and when polity is conceived as a device for executing the vital design of nature, the same tension will arise between polity and virtue as between nature and virtue. The final position, on the premises adopted by Smith, is a natural system of polity based upon preservation but in conflict with morality as Smith understands man to conceive it; which polity will not merely harmonize with but will utilize and grow upon the principle of nature's moral impartiality.

Let us continue our examination of Smith's system from the vantage of the cardinal virtues by noticing next his teaching on prudence. His formal consideration of prudence occurs in his treatise on the character of virtue as it affects the agent's own happiness as distinguished from that character of virtue which affects the happiness of others.[102] "The care of the health, of the fortune, of the rank and reputation of the individual, the objects upon which his comfort and happiness in this life are supposed principally to depend, is considered as the proper business of that virtue which is commonly called Prudence."[103] Since prudence is a virtue in the Smithian sense, it must by these terms be understood as relating to the acquisition of the external good of life in the manner most conformable to the sufferance of the world of spectators, i.e., to all other men. We might characterize it as decent but thoroughgoing care of one's external interest. Sobriety, industry, and frugality are the qualities that stand out in the portrait of prudence and that suggest it for the role of the commercial virtue par excellence.

Now Smith realized well that this conception of prudence differed largely from the one that had descended out of traditional writings. He acknowledged that prudence had earlier

---

102 "The qualities most *useful* to ourselves are, first of all, superior reason and understanding, by which are we capable of discerning the remote consequences all our actions, and of fore-seeing the advantage or detriment which is likely to result from them: and secondly, self-command, by which we are enabled to abstain from pleasure or to endure present pain, in order to obtain a greater pleasure, or to avoid a greater pain in some future time. In the union of those two qualities consists the virtue of prudence, of all the virtues that which is the most *useful* to the individual." *Theory of Moral Sentiments*, Pt. IV, Ch. II, p. 189. (Italics added.)

103 Ibid., Pt. VI, Sect. I, p. 213.

been conceived on an immensely wider scale (he called it "superior prudence"), as supposing "the utmost perfection of all the intellectual and of all the moral virtues," and as "the most perfect wisdom combined with the most perfect virtue."[104] This conception rejected, and prudence reconstrued as taking care of one's self, there disappear forthwith all traces of this virtue's traditional role as the rare habit of moral discrimination or understanding of how to act. Although it does not literally become by definition the attribute of every human being, it comes in some form within the reach of every creature that desires to live and prosper; and it does so the more particularly as Smith has affirmed of every man that he is fitter to take care of himself than of any other person.[105] We might say that, although not every man is perfectly prudent by any means, every man is sufficiently so for the purposes of nature, viz., for preservation or taking care of one's self. Not only, therefore, are all men substantially equal in their right to the means of preservation, but they are substantially equal in such mental power as is required to gain those means. This is not to say that all men have equal ability to enrich themselves, which no one would affirm, Smith least of all, but only that each man's passions inclining him so strongly in his own favor, and prudence proceeding from the selfish passions, as all of virtue does proceed from passion, every man can be

---

104 Ibid., Pt. VI, Sect. I, p. 216. Compare St. Thomas, *Summa Theologica*, second part of the second part, Q. 47, Art. 11, wherein is denied that prudence about one's own good is specifically the same as that which extends to the common good. Also, Aristotle, *Nicomachean Ethics*, 1143b23, "Practical wisdom (viz. prudence) is the quality of mind concerned with things just and noble and good for man."

105 Compare *Leviathan*, Chap. 8, wherein Hobbes, asserting the virtual equality of all men in the prerequisites of prudence, writes, "A plain husband-man is more Prudent in affaires of his own house, then a Privy Counsellor in the affaires of another man." See also Hobbes, *De Cive*, I, 9; *Leviathan*, Ch. 13, paragraph 2; and Descartes, *Discourse of Method*, p. 1.

relied upon not only to desire his living but to know the means to the modest substance thereof.

The reconstruction of prudence to exclude moral discrimination left a vacuum in the chamber of the excellences. If not prudence, then what attribute enables the individual to distinguish in detail between the better and the worse course of action? As the question arose out of what might be regarded as a degradation of prudence, so the answer is fittingly provided by the corresponding alteration of the category "wisdom." Adam Smith habitually associates wisdom and virtue, with the ultimate purpose of identifying them, as he explicitly does in writing, "The wise and virtuous man directs his principal attention to the (perfect) standard; the idea of exact *propriety* and perfection."[106] A view that Smith clarifies when he affirms that

> The wise man must support the propriety of his own conduct in health and sickness, in success and in disappointment, in the hour of fatigue and drowsy indolence, as well as in that of the most awakened attention. The most sudden and unexpected assaults of difficulty and distress must never surprise him. The injustice of other people must never provoke him to injustice. The violence of faction must never confound him. All the hardships and hazards of war must never either dishearten or appal him.[107]

What makes this passage decisive is not simply that it attributes moral virtue to the wise man, which is not unusual, but rather that it summarizes the whole of Smith's conception of the wise man's attributes. The general identification of wisdom with moral virtue is emphasized by the fact that the

---

106 *Theory of Moral Sentiments*, Pt. VI, Sect. III, p. 247. Italics not in original.

107 Ibid., Pt. VI, Sect. III, p. 249. Also Ibid., Pt. I, Sect. III, Ch. II, p. 57: For the man "so confirmed in wisdom and real philosophy, as to be satisfied that, while *the propriety of his conduct* renders him the just object of approbation, it is of little consequence though he be neither attended to, nor approved of . . . ." (My italics.)

Theory of Moral Sentiments contains literally nothing on the subject of intellectual virtue discernment of the means to literally "proper" conduct, is left as wisdom simply, both by affirmation and by default.

The general identification of true wisdom and moral virtue, however the latter is understood, inevitably calls to mind the Biblical principle having the same effect: that true wisdom, the best life, and indeed the highest human possibility, are all included in a qualification of action or behavior, through obedience to the will of God.[108] Indeed the Smithian teaching cannot fail to have much in common with every system that diminishes intellectual virtue or subordinates it to moral virtue; and the differences between Smithian and Biblical morality, great as they might be, seem to become less when account is taken of the similarity in their evaluation of morality by itself.

If the degradation of prudence left a void which was filled through the degradation of wisdom, what if anything filled the higher void left by the displacement of wisdom? The answer seems to be that the void came to be occupied by what we now know as "science." That is to say, the place formerly occupied by science conceived as search for the truth is taken, in Smith's writing, by science, in a quite different sense into which we must now briefly inquire.

Science or philosophy is what issues from man's response to the stimulus of wonder. Wonder, in turn, is a passion or sentiment[109] which is a species of pain or which is nearly related

---

108 Thus Ecclesiastes 12. 13: "The end of the matter, all having been heard: fear God, and keep his commandments; for this is the whole man." And Job 28. 12–28, especially verse 28; "Behold, the fear of the Lord, that is wisdom; and to depart from evil is understanding."

109 "The Principles Which Lead and Direct Philosophical Enquiries; Illustrated by the History of Astronomy," pp. 33, 34, 39, and throughout. This essay is one of three, all having the same title down to the semicolon. The two others end respectively "Illustrated by the History of the Ancient Physics" and "Illustrated by the History of the Ancient Logics and Metaphysics." There is no apparent reason why these three

to pain; for whereas "the mind takes pleasure in observing the *resemblances* that are discoverable betwixt different objects,"[110] wonder is "that uncertainty and anxious curiosity excited by [an unfamiliar object's] *singular* appearance, and by its *dissimilitude* with all the objects . . . hitherto observed."[111] Wonder is likewise aroused when the mind is confronted by "an unusual succession of things,"[112] the passion, in extreme circumstances mounting to the intolerable heights of "confusion and giddiness" or even "lunacy and distraction." Thus, to take note of similarity is pleasurable; to be conscious of dissimilarity excites wonder, and philosophy is a response to the prompting of painful passion.

If wonder is a painful passion, then science may be represented as an emollient, or a hedonic device having as its "ultimate end" "the repose and tranquility of the imagination."[113] The painfulness of wonder presents man with an urgent need for relief, with which he provides himself by creating those systems of science which render satisfaction as palliatives of troubled imaginations. "A system is an imaginary machine invented to connect together in the fancy those different movements and effects which are already ready in reality performed."[114] Of importance is the empathic sense in which Smith understood science to be human invention, as distinct from discovery. Eulogizing the Newtonian astronomy, Smith wrote, "And even we, while we have been endeavoring to represent all philosophical systems as mere inventions of the imagination, to connect together the otherwise disjointed and discordant phenomena of Nature, have insensibly been drawn in, to make use of language expressing the connecting principles of this one, as if they were the real chains which Nature

---

essays should not have been titled collectively The Theory of Intellectual Sentiments.

110 Ibid., p. 37.

111 Ibid., p. 40. Emphasis added in this and the previous reference.

112 Ibid., p. 42.

113 Ibid., p. 61. See also pp. 45–6; 75; 97.

114 Ibid., p. 66.

makes use of to bind together her several operations."[115] It follows that not its truth or falsity but its power to relieve man's anxiety is what is of the essence of science, for the repose of the imagination, not comprehension, is the ultimate end of science. Although, therefore, this conception of science seems to flow from the ancient premise that all men by nature desire to know, there is a profound difference between the traditional and the Smithian understanding of the grounds of science. In Aristotle's treatise *De Anima,* science or philosophy appears as the actualization of the universe, the realization or completion of the whole in the same sense as that in which the hearing of a tree's crashing down in the forest is the realization or completion of the sound connected with the fall. Unheard, the sound would be sound only in an ambiguous, partial, or incomplete sense. Similarly, rational consciousness of the universe provides that realization or completion without which the existence of the whole would be as partial as is that of the unheard sound. In brief, the completion or perfection of the universe requires science; science fulfills a requirement of the whole. It goes without saying that there is, from the traditional point of view, equally a sense in which the completion or perfection of man requires science. In this way, man and the universe are radically indispensable to each other.

From the Smithian point of view, science is exclusively a response to human requirements, and the truth of science therefore not of its essence, as has been said. It is idle to object that the preoccupation of science with "facts" implies the truth

---

115 Ibid., p. 105. Cf. Albert Einstein and L. Infeld, *The Evolution of Physics* (N.Y., 1942), p. 310: "Science is not just a collection of laws, a catalogue of unrelated facts. It is a creation of the human mind, with its freely invented ideas and concepts. Physical theories try to form a picture of reality and to establish its connection with the wide world of sense impressions. Thus the only justification for our mental structures is whether and in what way our theories form such a link." See also Sigmund Freud, *An Outline of Psychoanalysis,* (N.Y., 1940) pp. 105–6, containing a discussion of the limitations of science which includes the statement that "reality will always remain 'unknowable'."

of scientific conclusions; for the sense in which the truth is inferred from facts is in no sense superior to the sense in which what is a fact is inferred from the truth. There is a truth which must precede any fact, just as there is a truth which may follow from that fact. The absence of the prior truth must mar or obscure the posterior. But if truth is not of the essence of science (which of course is not to say that science and truth may not overlap) then science as a human activity ceases to differ in principle from many another human activity: it is not uniquely oriented upon the truth, but, like others, aims at quenching a passion – and not the passion most intimately connected with the preservation of life.

Restating the foregoing in brief, one might say that the proposition all men by nature desire to know may be affirmed as compatible with the premise "wonder is passion" and also with the premise "wonder is habit or disposition." But the construing of wonder as passion presupposes a commitment to the doctrine that men's passions define their nature, while the construing of wonder as a virtue implies that it is man's power to know what defines his nature.

The identification of science with the passional and hypothetical and its alienation from the true produce certain problems to which we must at least make reference. First it may be asked, how can self-conscious invention, avowedly different from truth, perform its function of assuaging wonder without implying the merger in principle of science and faith? Only his wonder will be assuaged by constructive science who believes it at the same time that he is conscious of its constructive character. He believes that which, and because, he wills to believe, i.e., he has faith; or else his wonder is not allayed. Of course, the endlessness of systems demonstrates that the wonder of the wise is never allayed; it cannot be allayed. Hence the end of science, if science is to be preserved as distinct from faith, as an intrinsically unattainable end so long as that end is conceived as the anesthetizing of painful wonder. Put differently, the end of science so conceived appears as a simultaneous satisfaction of the requirements of passion and reason – appeasement and also conviction. But no grounds exist for presuming in favor of the necessity of such a conjunction of satisfactions.

In addition, a question arises as to the worth or standing of science when science is assimilated in principle to non-science as a response to passion out of necessity. As identical in their origins, science and non-science are put upon a footing of equal worth. But science and non-science differ materially in respect of their ends, if not of their origins, and from this fact perhaps a ground may be discovered for understanding the differential place of science.

The end of science is described by Smith as the repose of the imagination, which means that the ends of science and of nature do not coincide. The incongruity of purpose between the natural and the scientific points directly and insistently to the problem of the worth or standing of science – with respect to the natural and hence in general. For if nature and science aim in different directions, man cannot long escape the necessity of choosing to pursue the one end to the exclusion of the other, and his choice will presuppose an order in their choice-worthiness. I believe that the outline of Adam Smith's position in this respect may be given in summary form as follows. We have seen[116] that Smith regarded the moral as superior in worth to the intellectual – duty as superior to contemplation, or moral virtue as superior to understanding. We have seen further[117] that Smith's appreciation of morality must be understood as containing a discrimination between the morality prescribed by nature simply and the higher moral order produced and preferred by man. But the favorite end of nature corresponds to the end of the natural moral order. We might therefore say that the human moral order, the natural moral order, and philosophy or science are ranked by Smith in that sequence from highest to lowest.

The practical effects of such doctrine are broad and deep, including as they do the proposition that the life of contemplation cannot be represented as superior in principle to the life of concern with the things of preservation. Some such argument is indispensable to an advocacy of the commercialization of the world. It is the necessary condition for the

116 Above, pp. 9 ff.
117 Above, pp. 43 ff.

replacement of excellence as the constant goal of polity. Such a premise wanting, the argument that the way to happiness is legion, indeed comprehensive, would be difficult, perhaps impossible to sustain.

Remaining at last is the problem which perplexes all systems that systematically depreciate science or philosophy, namely, what is the standing of that very science, a dominating element of which is the depreciation of science. Such a science undertakes to arbitrate between science and non-science as if it itself possessed only so much authority as is necessary to divest itself of authority. But it is clear that the authority to renounce authority implies also the authority to retain it, and whatever concedes the former implies the latter. The arbitrator cannot abdicate its function in favor of a party to a cause but only to another coequal, who then acquires the title of arbitrator. The self-disqualification of a judge implies not the impossibility of giving judgment but the availability of a judge better qualified to give it. Every science that depreciates science, Smith's of course included, argues by its example, though not by its precept, that there must be a suprascientific science of science which is not subject to the limitations of science. How far this is absurd, in what sense it argues again the identity of faith and highest science, and in what degree it ignores the fact that the indefeasible superiority of philosophy is guaranteed by the truth that whatever authoritatively contemplates the worth of philosophy is itself philosophy we must eschew as questions not within our present province; and on this note conclude our discussion of the immediate problem of wisdom in Adam Smith and the bearing it has upon his teaching.

There is yet another lesson to be learned from Smith's account of the four cardinal virtues, this one drawn from his teaching concerning self-command. Of self-command he wrote that it is "not only itself a great virtue, but from it all the other virtues seem to derive their principal lustre."[118] The reason for the primacy of self-command is that, when the passions obstruct the practice of prudence, justice, and benevolence, it is the force of self-command that reinforces the virtues

---

118 *Theory of Moral Sentiments*, Pt. VI, Sect. III, p. 241.

and enables them to become manifest despite the passions. Thus the *sine qua non* of all virtue is the repression of passionate impulses towards vice. Smith classifies the passions according to an ancient principle: some of them focus about anger and fear, the others about sensual gratification in one sense or another; the former corresponding to the irascible, the latter to the concupiscible passions, although Smith does not employ this traditional terminology. He affirms that the ancients knew as fortitude the virtue by which the irascible passions were subdued, and as temperance that by which the concupiscible were controlled. He himself conceived both orders of passion to be in the jurisdiction of the virtue "self-command." In effect, prudence, justice, and benevolence are possible only through or by self-command. If self-command means "control of all the passions," then all the (moral) virtues, and surely prudence, justice, and benevolence, can be reduced to self-command. In a radical sense, self-command becomes the only virtue. But we have seen indicated above the intimate connection between self-command and pleasure and pain. It will be recalled that we noted self-command to be the quality "by which we are enabled to abstain from present pleasure or to endure present pain, in order to obtain a greater pleasure, or to avoid a greater pain in some future time." Combining the elements of the argument to this point, we may say that all virtue and the maximization of pleasure meet in self-command, leaving us with the idea that virtue is a form of maximization of pleasures and minimization of pains. But virtue defined as intrinsically pleasurable must ultimately seek pleasurable ends; or conversely, virtue must be oriented upon pleasurable ends if it is to be intelligible as intrinsically pleasurable. To evaluate Smith's position fully, we should be obliged to examine his conception of pleasure, or what ends are pleasurable, which we cannot and need not do here. As a generally hedonistic doctrine, however, Smith's is open to such objections, centering on the occasional tension between virtue and pleasure, as have often been raised against theories of this description, into which we need not enter now.

For reasons that will emerge as we proceed, we turn next to the general effect produced upon Smith's system by the character of his doctrines concerning pride. These doctrines will not be entirely intelligible, nor will the order of society corresponding to them be so, without a view of earlier teachings and orders which they supplanted. In antiquity, pride was regarded as a virtue, in particular as the virtue belonging to the excellent man who properly esteems himself highly. Pride was itself considered admirable because, correctly understood, it was inseparable from the highest virtue and reflected that reasonable, sincere, and high-minded consciousness of excellence without which excellence itself is impossible. The excellent man, suitably proud, comported himself with the dignity and bearing which tradition attaches to the word "aristocratic," with that imperturbable gravity that compels respect, and which, as it was described by Aristotle, suggested to Adam Smith the demeanor of the proud Spaniard.[119] The proud man knows himself to be deserving of honor, and his deportment evokes it, yet the essence of pride as anciently understood having been the true superiority and hence self-sufficiency of the excellent man, he disdains to seek anything at the hands of others; and so, strangely, "not even towards honor does he bear himself as if it were a very great thing."[120] As for power and wealth, which are desirable for the sake of honor, his superiority will not allow him to exert himself in their pursuit "as if they were very great things."

It is worth observing that this attitude towards pride was rejected alike by Biblical morality and by the moral philosophers among whom Adam Smith must be included. The grounds of the rejection by both Biblical and secular moralists coincide at least to this extent: that both begin by denying the possibility of that excellence which justifies pride and by its presence distinguishes pride from ridiculous vanity. We need say no more of the Biblical morality than that it commences with man's sinfulness and conceives him as imperfect all the days of his life on earth. Adam Smith reasons to the same conclusion from the premise that men may judge of themselves according to two standards, the one representing perfection

119 Ibid., Pt. VI, Sect. III, p. 258.
120 *Nicomachean Ethics*, 1224a17.

simply, and the other the modest level of accomplishment actually attained in the world. By the latter standard there are indeed some men who might view themselves with a degree of satisfaction; but by the former, which is ultimately the only standard, every human being must fall far short of that measure of excellence which alone could vindicate pride. And even as the best of men must fall short of true excellence, so will it be found that the "best" are superior only in certain departments of life, and in others are less than other men. The wise and virtuous man's "whole mind, in short, is deeply impressed, his whole behavior and deportment are distinctly stamped with the character of real modesty; with that of a very moderate estimation of his own merit, and, at the same time, with a very full sense of the merit of other people."[121]

Whereas pride was formerly regarded as virtuous because it exalted excellence, it is regarded by Smith as vicious,[122] since the perfection that might justify proud self-estimation is literally impossible. For Smith, the virtuous degree of self-esteem is not pride but modesty or even, more exactly, humility.[123]

And yet we are prevented from concluding that Smith regarded pride or everything akin to pride as simply bad; for it must be remembered that that propriety of passion in man which constitutes his excellence is inspired by an impulse to support his dignity, in effect to avoid the contempt of other men and to gain their regard.[124] It is impossible to separate

---

121 *Theory of Moral Sentiments*, Pt. VI, Sect. III, p. 248. See, generally, ibid., Pt. VI, Sect. III, pp. 246–9; Pt. I, Sect. I, Ch. V, p. 25–6.

122 Pride and vanity are referred to as "those two vices," ibid., Pt. VI, Sect. III, p. 255. With this compare Hobbes, *Leviathan*, Ch. 15. The violation of the (ninth) law of nature is Pride.

123 Smith affirms that, if the exactly proper degree of self-estimation is to be missed, it is more virtuous to err in the direction of humility than of vanity. *Theory of Moral Sentiments*, Pt. VI, Sect. III, p. 247. Aristotle, however, writes, "undue humility is more opposed to pride than vanity is," *Nicomachean Ethics*, 1125a33.

124 Among many other passages bearing on this matter, the following stands out as typical: "[the man] who feels . . . what the dignity of his own character requires . . . is alone the real man of

entirely the impulse to support one's dignity from pride in some sense. Smith acknowledges this when he writes, "We frequently say of a man, that he is too proud, or that he has too much noble pride, ever to suffer himself to do a mean thing. Pride is, in this case, confounded with magnanimity."[125]

Smith's principle is that there is a radical difference between pride and magnanimity (although the difference, in truth, is not so profound that the two cannot be identified in common understanding). We may, however, understand the basis of the distinction as follows: Smith has redefined pride to mean sincerely but erroneously conceived self-estimation *in excess of merit*.[126] Ultimately, every man who esteems himself highly must be guilty of pride for reasons relating to the literal impossibility of imperfection, as stated above. Pride, therefore, is vice. But what of that sort of self-estimation in virtue of which a man will not tolerate baseness in himself? Upon this regard for the requirements of one's own dignity, which we might term self-respect, is based the "magnanimity" that is the source of propriety and hence of virtue itself.[127] Evidently

virtue, the only real and proper object of love, respect, and admiration." *Theory of Moral Sentiments*, Pt. VI, Sect. III, p. 245. Also, conjoined in the same place, are "dignity and propriety," the latter admitted to be "the real essence of virtue."

125 *Theory Of Moral Sentiments*, Pt. VI, Sect. III, p. 258. The import of this is precisely comparable to Hobbes, *Leviathan*, Ch. 14 (Molesworth pp. 128–9): "The force of words, being, as I have formerly noted, too weak to hold men to the performance of their covenants; there are in man's nature but two imaginable helps to strengthen it. And those are either a fear of breaking their word; (cf. *Theory of Moral Sentiments*, Pt. I, Sect. I, Ch. I, p. 13) or a glory, or pride in appearing not to need to break it. This latter is a generosity too rarely found to be presumed on, especially in the pursuers of wealth, command, or sensual pleasure; which are the greatest part of mankind. The passion to be reckoned upon, is fear. . .."

126 *Theory of Moral Sentiments*, Pt. VI, Sect. III, p. 255.

127 Cf. ibid., Pt. IV, Ch. II, p. 191: "When to the interest of this other person, therefore, they sacrifice their own, they accommodate themselves to the sentiments of the spectator, and by an effort of

there is an ambiguity in the phenomenon of self-regard, in that it includes both self-esteem and self-respect, the one seeking honor and the other seeking love[128] in recognition of virtue, – the one vicious and the other virtuous. Whether this dichotomy could finally be maintained is a very difficult question, one which we are fortunately not called upon to answer. However, even as upon this reasoning we should have expected, for Smith the reward of virtue is not honor, as it was conceived to be in the system that recognized pride as virtuous, but rather "love." It is in this fashion that pride comes to be related to magnanimity as its corruption.

We might express the relation between Smithian pride and magnanimity in another way which will emphasize its peculiar bearing upon our own subject. The self-regard that was anciently called pride, and was thought to be a virtue, was connected with the genuine superiority of the extraordinary man. It might be thought of as the symbol of superiority and therefore of human inequality. The "magnanimous" self-regard that is the precondition (not the crown) of virtue in the Smithian system, supports a dignity which is the equal dignity of all men as such, figuratively confronted by all other men, viz. by the whole world of impartial spectators.[129] Virtue is known by the consensus of "all," and is intelligible as the impulse to conduct which meets the vital requirements of "all" equally. The self-regard which restrains a man from vice resembles the sturdy, simple instinct to preserve one's good name and to avoid one's neighbors' contempt rather than to incline towards honor. Without doubt this makes demands

magnanimity act according to those views of things which they feel must naturally occur to any third person."
128 Love is cited as the reward of virtue in too many passages to mention. See, e.g., *Theory of Moral Sentiments*, Pt. I, Sect. II, Ch. IV, p. 38–9, Pt. III, Ch. III, p. 152; Pt. III, Ch. V, p. 167; Pt. VI, Sect. II, Ch. I, p. 225; Pt. VI, Sect. II, Ch. III, p. 236, etc.
129 That magnanimity is the property of men as such and not of extraordinary men is indicated by Smith's attribution of magnanimity to savages as their peculiar characteristic. Ibid., Pt. V, Ch. II, p. 206.

upon men, but it makes demands which eventuate in the virtues of perfect equality rather than the virtues of inequality either of rank or of honor. We see this clearly in Smith's rejection of the virtues of the great as such, which he terms "arts" and contrasts with the genuine virtues of knowledge, industry, patience and self-denial.[130] In these ways the virtues of unequal rank give way to the virtues of humble equality while honor gives place to love as the desideratum of man; and the entire process is summarized in the rejection of pride as virtue.

We cannot leave the field whereon honor was defeated by the virtues that flow from the requirements of preservation without referring to the bearing of Smith's treatment of pride on the tension between nature and morality already mentioned. In a striking passage,[131] Smith argues that when man is called upon to suffer the pain that comes with heeding the requirements of dignity, he is compensated for his virtue with the esteem of himself and others; but

> by [Nature's] unalterable laws, however, he still suffers; and the recompense which she bestows, though very considerable, is not sufficient completely to compensate the sufferings which those laws inflict. Neither is it fit that it should. If it did completely compensate them, he could, from self-interest, have no motive for avoiding an accident which must necessarily diminish his utility both to himself and to society; and Nature, from her parental care of both, meant that he should anxiously avoid all such accidents.

In other words, the self-love which is the desire for self-preservation was meant by nature to prevail over the self-love which is self-respect and which corresponds to the requirements of dignity – a doctrine that accords with our conclusion as to the reason for Smith's radical distinction between pride and magnanimity.

The point to which the argument has led us is this: Smith has raised moral over intellectual virtue while in a manner of

---

130 Ibid., Pt. I, Sect. III, Ch. II, p. 54.
131 Ibid., Pt. III, Ch. III, p. 148.

speaking expunging from morality pride and the proud virtues. At the same time, therefore, that humility is inscribed among the virtues, wisdom, separated from the truth, is disgraced as the goal of life; while pride is banished, making excellence compatible with eager seeking after the good. We cannot avoid noticing the anomaly that the elevation of moral over intellectual virtue, proceeding from man's abdication of his greatest claim to distinction in the universe, results in a lowering of the very level of morality through its effect upon pride. Or in other words, by a reconstruction of nature, human life has been given a new direction upon a new plane, and at the same time, indeed necessarily, excellence has been conceived to include the unabashed pursuit of the new good. To correspond with the prescription by nature of preservation as the goal of life, the best man is conceived as the one who preserves himself "best," not only most securely and commodiously, but also in such a way as not to obstruct the preservation of the rest of mankind, his equals in humanity. As must be the case, the idea of the best man must accord with the idea of the best life; the best man is he who lives the best life. The best man incorporates excellence, and the best life is best because it leads to happiness, which is a way of saying that excellence and happiness cannot really be separated. In virtue of this truth we shall conclude this survey of the first principles of Adam Smith's political and moral doctrine with a view of his teaching concerning excellence and happiness.

Smith's expressions on the substance of perfection are relatively few in number[132] and are mutually consistent. They may be represented by the passage already cited, "to feel much for others and little for ourselves, . . . to restrain our selfish, and indulge benevolent affections, constitutes the perfection of human nature."[133] The corresponding passages describing happiness[134] may be typified by two: "The chief

---

132 *Theory of Moral Sentiments*, Pt. I, Sect. I, Ch. V, p. 25; Pt. I, Sect. III, Ch. I, p. 45; Pt. III, Ch. III, p. 152; Pt. III, Ch. V, p. 163; Pt. VI, Sect. III, p. 237.

133 Ibid., Pt. I, Sect. I, Ch. V, p. 25.

134 Ibid., e.g., Pt. I, Sect. II, Ch. IV, p. 39; Pt. I, Sect. II, Ch. V, p. 41; Pt.

part of human happiness arises from the consciousness of being beloved,"[135] and,

> In what constitutes the real happiness of human life, [the humble] are in no respect inferior to those who would seem so much above them. In ease of the body and peace of the mind, all the different ranks of life are nearly upon a level, and the beggar who suns himself by the side of the highway, possesses all that security which kings are fighting for.[136]

Smith's view is, indeed, that the excellence of man is to be understood as that moral virtue which, as it comes into being through the offices of sympathy, so is it accompanied by the pleasures of being the object of sympathy; which pleasures are known as happiness. Perfection is moral virtue or "goodness" in its homeliest sense, and happiness is the tranquil pleasure of being loved for goodness.

Both from this description and from Smith's own figure of the beggar and the king, excellence and happiness appear to exist within the reach of "all." We need not go to the length of affirming that all men are excellent and happy; we need only admit that the ideals of perfection and happiness are compatible with the way of life of all or almost all, viz. of every human type. There is almost no single goal or good the pursuit of which is incompatible with excellence and happiness; and since the lifelong pursuit of an end is what is meant by the "way of life," we may say that Adam Smith has aimed at divorcing the concepts of perfection and happiness from the problem of the way of life or the goal, and binding them instead to the problem of the manner of living or the manner of pursuing the goal, irrespective of the nature of the goal to which the life is tending. But the manner of living is the morality or immorality of living, and a good manner of living is for

---

I, Sect. III, Ch. I, p. 45; Pt. III, Ch. I, p. 113; Pt. III, Ch. V, p. 166; Pt. IV, Ch. I, p. 185; Pt. VI, Sect. II, Ch. I, p. 225.

135 Ibid., Pt. I, Sect. II, Ch. V, p. 41.

136 Ibid., Pt. IV, Ch. I, p. 185.

Adam Smith moral virtue, meaning by that the pursuit of preservation while hindering no one else in the like pursuit.

Try as we may, we shall not escape the consequences of Smith's exaltation of moral virtue. It is the nature of moral virtue to belong to the genus of means rather than of ends. Morality is a way of acting or living; but action and life must have some proper end, or the meaning of excellence in life and action begins to slip away from the mind's grasp. Surely the end cannot itself be the action, or the living, or even the manner of the acting or living, apart from the goal of the entire process. Yet that it is so must be the inference from the far-reaching principle that happiness is a feeling, and excellence a condition, that lie in the path of every way of life.

CHAPTER II
FREEDOM, HISTORY, AND THE COMMERCIAL ORDER OF POLITY

We have set out to understand the passage of Adam Smith's first principles into a system of society; or, conversely, the theoretical genesis of commercial society. Societies experience a coming into being and a passing away, to which is apposite the matter of those fateful pages with which Plato concludes *The Republic*: at their politic as at their moral inception, men collective, like men individual, seek out an end and a way of life, bestial or exalted or mediocre, the incidents of which, but not the guiding principle, must be unknown to them when they choose. The choice is free, but once made there is no turning aside. And the choice is made at inception, which corresponds with the fact that each being's individuality or existence as proper individual proceeds from and begins with his difference from all others, which difference is intelligible in terms of the separate end or function of each. In a sense, then, the individual, man or society, does not begin to exist as individual until it is launched, or has launched itself, toward its singular end by its own proper decision.

The bearing of this upon our subject is twofold, and arises from the facts, first, that Smith's teaching upon society includes principles of the coming into being of societies or polities; and second, as is by now generally admitted, Smith by his writings was himself seeking to cause a new polity to come into being. When we take under consideration the passage of Smith's general principles into a system of society, we find forced upon our attention the end or way of life to be chosen and also the process of coming into being of the society based upon the new rule. We shall examine the latter subject first.

Smith speculated upon the career of systems of society considered as systems, and emerged with a type of philosophy of history. His philosophy of history is founded in his description of the hierarchy of grades of social organization and the characteristics of the grades[1] as they could in fact have existed in the world; there is nothing about them which is intrinsically "hypothetical." Most elementary, "the lowest and rudest state of society" is the nation of hunters, in which "there is properly neither sovereign nor commonwealth."[2] Next higher among the rude societies is that of the animal husbandmen or nomadic shepherds, which "nations have all chiefs or sovereigns."[3] Next are "those nations of husbandmen who have little foreign commerce, and no other manufactures but those coarse and household ones which almost every private family prepares for its own use."[4] And finally there is "a more advanced stage of society," recognizable as that of the modern west, with agriculture, manufacture, and commerce. The character of "civilized" is reserved exclusively to the last mentioned stage.[5]

From this account we may infer a number of Smith's principles relating to society. In the first place, this summary sketch is strikingly and entirely apolitical in its terms. (a) The criterion of rudeness or civilization, i.e. of excellence, is the mode of economic or "social" organization, although tradition might have led us to expect a discussion in terms of democracy, aristocracy, or monarchy, and so on. (b) Hunters are described as living in society, yet having "neither sovereign nor commonwealth," by which is emphasized Smith's radical

---

1   *Wealth of Nations*, Bk. V, Ch. I.
2   Ibid., Bk. V, Ch. I, Pt. I, p. 689–90.
3   Ibid., Bk. V, Ch. I, Pt. I, p. 691.
4   Ibid., Bk. V, Ch. I, Pt. I, p. 692.
5   Ibid., Bk. V, Ch. I, Pt. I, pp. 694–5.

distinction between polity and society, of which we shall presently have more to say. (c) And in the same vein, we are reminded that the line of distinction between rudeness and civilization is drawn, not between pre-political and political existence, nor yet between pre-social and social (an uninteresting distinction in Smith's terms, since existence anterior to "society" seems unintelligible) but rather between all economic (scil. "social") forms less than the highest on the one side, and the highest form on the other.[6] Smith's dissociation of civilization and "political" life reminds us of the absence from his writings of any reference whatever to the famous distinction between the State of Nature and the State of Civil Society. The transition from the former to the latter was understood by those who employed it to coincide with the passage of man from a solitary to a social and *hence* political existence, since society or living together was thought to be inseparable from sovereignty or commonwealth. But Smith substitutes for the essentially political transition from State of Nature to State of Civil Society the apolitical distinction rudeness – civilization, which implies not merely the distinction of polity and society but the subordination of the former to the latter, and the general reduction of "polity" to the service of "society" for the sake of "civilization."

We must try to understand Smith's position from his own vantage. The distinguishing criterion, or essence of society is disclosed by Smith's summary history to be the manner of procuring the means of existence, what we speak of now as economic organization. The stages of society are identified as distinct forms of economic organization, and change in economic organization not only marks but is, change in "society" and in the level of excellence thereof. Society by these lights is the concourse of men viewed as a means for pursuing the requisites of preservation,[7] while polity is the same concourse

6   Thus we are astonished to read of the distinction between "civilization" and the condition of "the little agrarian states of ancient Greece." Ibid., Bk. V, Ch. I, Pt. I, p. 695.

7   Indeed, the very origins of society were thought by Smith to be profoundly connected with man's economic requirements. It is

viewed as the means of distributing the powers and duties of rule. In a sense, though, *the* political problem is the problem of who shall rule, meaning by that, who is best qualified to rule for the sake of the supreme end sought by political life. To subordinate that to any other problem of common life, e.g., to what we might call *the* social problem, namely what system of organization supplies the means of preservation in greatest abundance, is at least upon the face of it to imply the unimportance of "who shall rule" in comparison with "what is the most productive economy," and by implication, the elevation of preservation to the highest place in human consideration. But though this teaching of the *Wealth of Nations* seems clearly enough to subordinate polity to economy, we must regard the subordination as at least unexplained, and surely provisional, until we explore Smith's political teaching more largely. Suffice it for the present to say that it would be incorrect to infer that Smith regarded the political order as unambiguously of secondary importance.

The second of Smith's principles inferable from his summary history, but even more visible in certain other passages to be considered, relates to the mechanism by which men pass from one historical phase to another, or to the coming into being of a form of society. It might be supposed that in considering their life in common, men would ponder the benefits and the costs of their communal arrangement and would alter or strengthen it in accordance with a rational principle or deliberate choice, or at least with a choice based upon an ele-

---

men's misguided devotion to wealth "which first prompted them to cultivate the ground, to build houses, to found cities and commonwealths, and to invent and improve all the sciences and arts, which ennoble and embellish human life; which have entirely changed the whole face of the globe, have turned the rude forests of nature into agreeable and fertile plains, and made the trackless and barren ocean a new fund of subsistence, and the great high road of communication to the different nations of the earth. The earth by these labours of mankind has been obliged to redouble her natural fertility, and to maintain a greater multitude of inhabitants." *Theory of Moral Sentiments*, Pt. IV, Ch. II, p. 183–4.

ment of rationality somewhere, even one separated from the apparent choosers by a number of stages of rhetoric. But the element of rational choice in the process of social evolution is precisely what Smith denies. Instead, the institutions of society are described as the direct outgrowths of certain material conditions of life which Smith summarizes as "the state of property and manners" prevailing at the time in question.[8] Consider the history of Europe. The disintegration of the Roman empire left Europe in chaos, from which it was at least partially redeemed by the action of the magnates who appropriated literally all of the land allodially, and with it gained supreme control of the livelihood and hence of the allegiance of all the land's inhabitants.[9] The feudal organization of society was simply a moderation of the system inherited from post-imperial allodialism.[10] The supreme importance of the possessors of land may be said to have been thrust upon them by the conditions of the age, in that, there being no noteworthy manufacture or commerce to tempt their appetites with luxuries, they were obliged to cause their wealth to be consumed outright by the surrounding crowds of men who became at once their retainers and the essence of their power.[11] Not only is it true that the authority and jurisdiction of the medieval lords "flowed from the state of property and manners" prevailing, but "such effects must always flow from such causes."[12] We may say, therefore, that Smith accounts for the state of Europe in the middle ages by reference to the engrossment of the land in a few hands and the absence of manufactures or foreign commerce, but not from legal enactment representing rational choice.

---

8   *Wealth of Nations*, Bk. III, Ch. IV, p. 417.

9   Ibid., Bk. III, Ch. II, p. 381–2, ff; III, IV, p. 416.

10   Ibid., Bk. III, Ch. IV, p. 416.

11   Ibid., Bk. III, Ch. IV, pp. 412–5; Bk. V, Ch. I, Pt. III, Art. III, p. 803; Bk. V, Ch. III, p. 907. Cf. J. A. Froude, *History of England*, Vol. I, p. 91: "The higher classes have gained in luxury what they have lost in power."

12   *Wealth of Nations*, Bk. III, Ch. IV, p. 416.

The disappearance of the medieval system is accounted for by identical reasons:

> But what all the violence of the feudal institutions could never have effected, the silent and insensible operation of foreign commerce and manufactures gradually brought about. These gradually furnished the great proprietors with something for which they could exchange the whole surplus produce of their lands, and which they could consume themselves without sharing it either with tenants or retainers. All for ourselves, and nothing for other people, seems, in every age of the world, to have been the vile maxim of the masters of mankind. As soon, therefore, as they could find a method of consuming the whole value of their rents themselves, they had no disposition to share them with any other persons. For a pair of diamond buckles perhaps, or for something as frivolous and useless, they exchanged the maintenance, or what is the same thing, the price of the maintenance of a thousand men for a year, and with it the whole weight and authority which it could give them. The buckles, however, were to be all their own, and no other human creature was to have any share of them; whereas in the more ancient method of expence they must have shared with at least a thousand people. With the judges that were to determine the preference, this difference was perfectly decisive; and thus, for the gratification of the most childish, the meanest and the most sordid of all vanities, they gradually bartered their whole power and authority.[13]

If we look to that other tremendous phenomenon of European history, the secularization of the order of society, we find the same reasoning employed in assigning causes.

> In the ancient state of Europe, before the establishment of arts and manufactures, the wealth of the clergy gave them the same sort of influence over the com-

---

13   Ibid., Bk. III, Ch. IV, pp. 418–9.

mon people, which that of the great barons gave them over their respective vassals, tenants, and retainers. In the great landed estates, which the mistaken piety both of princes and private persons had bestowed upon the church, jurisdictions were established of the same kind with those of the great barons; and for the same reason. . . . The quantity [of their produce] exceeded greatly what the clergy could themselves consume; and there were neither arts nor manufactures for the produce of which they could exchange the surplus. The clergy could derive advantage from this immense surplus in no other way than by employing it, as the great barons employed the like surplus of their revenues, in the most profuse hospitality, and in the most extensive charity.[14]

And for the conclusion of the tale,

The gradual improvements of arts, manufactures, and commerce, the same causes which destroyed the power of the great barons, destroyed in the same manner, through the greater part of Europe, the whole temporal power of the clergy. . . . The ties of interest, which bound the inferior ranks of people to the clergy, were in this manner gradually broken and dissolved.[15]

---

14 Ibid., Bk. V, Ch. I, Pt. III, Art. III, pp. 800–1.
15 Ibid., Bk. V, Ch. I, Pt. III, Art. III, p. 803. This process must not be mistaken for the Protestant Reformation, the power of which is accounted for otherwise: "The preachers of the reformed religion possessed too in a much higher degree than their adversaries, all the arts of popularity and of gaining proselytes, arts which the lofty and dignified sons of the church had long neglected, as being to them in a great measure useless. The reason of the new doctrines recommended them to some, their novelty to many; the hatred and contempt of the established clergy to a still greater number; but the zealous, passionate, and fanatical, though frequently coarse, acid rustic, eloquence with which they were almost every where inculcated, recommended them to by far the greatest number." Ibid., Bk. V, Ch. I, Pt. III, Art. III, p. 806.

And if we wish one more illustration of the secondary role in history of rational principles of right as causes, let us consider briefly Adam Smith's account of the origins of American independence:

> The leading men of America, like those of all other countries, desire to preserve their own importance. They feel, or imagine, that if their assemblies, which they are fond of calling parliaments, and of considering as equal in authority to the parliament of Great Britain, should be so far degraded as to become the humble ministers and executive officers of that parliament, the greater part of their own importance would be at an end. They have rejected, therefore, the proposal of being taxed by parliamentary requisition, and like other ambitious and high-spirited men, have rather chosen to draw the sword in defence of their own importance.[16]

It should be realized, however, that although there is a historical arena in which choice and right are irrelevant, i.e., absent, Smith has by no means ejected choice in general from the realm of history. Book III of the *Wealth of Nations* finds Smith discussing the "natural" progress of opulence, or the sequential stages of society indicated by nature, culminating in the natural order of society; but the same Book III is devoted in large measure to describing the ways in which the natural order of things was inverted by the policy of Europe.[17] Two important inferences follow from this; first, human choice and decision, flowing admittedly not from reason but from the clash of passions, produce the institutions that shape society at any time, and those institutions may be contrary to nature, which remains as the nominal standard; and second, since history produces "inversions" of the true or natural order, history is not itself the legitimation of the order that exists by the fiat of history, but must give place to some other standard of excellence. That standard, if it is nature, will differ from the

16   Ibid., Bk. IV, Ch. VII, Pt. III, pp. 622.
17   Ibid., Bk. III, 1, p. 380 ff.

simply best by as much as the tension between nature and morality[18] will imply; but it will compensate for its moral deficiencies in ways that will appear. Since history is not the rational expression of nature but in principle may conflict with nature, there arises the need for a statement of the strictly natural, which of course is the substance of the *Wealth of Nations*, a book that delivers the truth about nature.

If we were obliged to reduce Smith's historical teaching to a single, simple proposition, we might recur to the following formula: The arrangement of the social forms that rule men's common existence is a direct outgrowth of the facts of an historical background; and those facts exert their influence through their power to excite the passions of groups of men who bring forth the next arrangement of society (and even polity) by their maneuverings on behalf of their interest. The process is finite only in the sense in which nature works to an end,[19] and of course the finitude of the historical process is defined by the "end" of nature. Thus we observe that the highest form of social organization which is mentioned by Smith is "civilization," or commercial society founded upon the elaborate division of labor. This social form is highest (not in the sense of "noblest") precisely because it best suits the end of nature, namely the preservation of man's existence. Yet there is nothing in the nature of things which will or might "inevitably" lead to the coming into being of the natural or most expedient social arrangement.

It seems, however, that the most important meaning that can be attached to the principle of the historical subordination of polity to society is that the facts of society rather than the facts of polity govern man's life in community. Thus civilization is thought to be connected with the commercial organization of society, not with, say, monarchy as such. The implication is that, in order to procure civilization, what is necessary is the "social" fact of commerce, or in other words a certain state of property and manners, rather than any particular distribution of authority, honor, and so on. The important possi-

18 See above, p. 43 ff.
19 See above, pp. 2 ff._

bility that this is indeed the key to Smith's entire teaching will
be discussed in the next chapter.

The second question connected with the etiology of societies is, what social arrangement ought to be or deserves to be
caused to come into being? The question is intelligible only if
the end sought by society itself be known (and in the present
context, if it be borne in mind that the end for society exists in
Smith's teaching on several levels).[20]

One can make recommendations as to the nature of the
society that should be brought into being only with reference
to the reason for society in general. We have already seen one
of Adam Smith's answers to the question, What is the end of
society? Society is an instrument of nature which, like all
instruments, seeks the end of its principal, in this case the
preservation of life. The best society, or the one that should be
cultivated into being, is that which best provides the means of
life, which of course include abundance of things needful both
to be consumed and to be employed in warding off attack
from without. It is by this principle that we may at least in part
understand Smith's advocacy of a form of society which is jus-
tified as being most productive of wealth and most conducive
to armed power of defense. What we must now consider is,
what form does society have when it conduces to wealth and
armed might better than does any other social form; or, what
is the complete commercial society?

* * *

The first watchword of the natural order might be said to
be Freedom and Equality, two intimately related terms which
require definition. We observed in Chapter I the importance to
Smith's moral philosophy of the principle of the radical equal-

---

20 By this is meant that there is a distinction between the ends
    which his *theory* seems to indicate as the objectives of society, and
    certain ends which, though not avowed, seem to be what Smith
    was really aiming at by the application to practice of his theoret-
    ical objectives. But the full exposition of this matter would best
    wait for the next chapter.

ity of all human beings in their passion-born right to seek their preservation. But their right to seek the means of life is meaningless unless they are confirmed in possession of those things which they have lawfully acquired; or in other words, natural equality is outraged by insecurity in possession. It is alike outraged by any impediment upon the fullest exercise by individuals of their self-preservative powers, within the limits set by the requirements of others. Indeed justice itself has been defined simply as the virtue of moderating one's efforts in one's own behalf according to the vital requirements of others as such. The absence of any such impediment upon the self-preservative powers is, however, an aspect of freedom as we now commonly understand it, which aspect is called freedom of contract. Freedom of contract is a defensible principle only in virtue of two of Smith's fundamental tenets: (1) that all men are sufficiently prudent in their own affairs; and (2) that justice is created by contract, or in other words that any exchange to which sane men commit themselves cannot be unjust since each is acquiring something which he values at least as highly as that which he gives up. And just as the absence of impediments to the full exercise of the self-preservative powers constitutes one element of "freedom" so does confirmation in possession, or guarantee against deprivation of goods, constitute or at least imply the other element of "freedom." For it is certain that no ruler but an absolute ruler could safely violate the property of his subjects, and the distance of the institutions from absolutism is therefore a part of security in possession, which is the reason for the association of security in property with free polity. To obtain full confirmation in possession and full right to exercise the self-preservative powers, what is needed are the institutions of free polity. Examining these, we shall in effect be examining what Smith puts forth as the necessary conditions for the existence of commercial society.

It is therefore not surprising to find considerable evidence of Smith's preference for "republicanism" above all other regimes. He was as overt in his arguments as a reasonably prudent man might have been, though he never went to the length of making positive proposals in this regard for his own country. Much of his advocacy of "republicanism" is implied by his reiterated praise of those aspects of Dutch life which were supposedly assignable to republican institutions. Thus Holland, one of the "richest and most industrious countries," continues to prosper from "peculiar circumstances,"[21] which we learn are "the republican form of government."[22] Holland is held up as the standard and the type of the commercial polity.[23] The digression on the Bank of Amsterdam is largely an encomium on Dutch prudence. The burghers of Amsterdam are "attentive and parsimonious."[24] The republic of Holland is "wise."[25] Holland approaches nearest in Europe to freedom of trade.[26] And so on.

Precisely what Smith meant by republicanism is partly in doubt, but useful intimations of it are not scarce. It will be remembered that Holland was a "republic" with an hereditary chief or stadholder who belonged to an hereditary nobility; wherefore Madison and Hamilton denied that the Netherlands existed on a republican principle at all, claiming instead that they were a confederation of aristocracies ruled by a prince in chief command of their army and navy. Supreme authority was not derived from the people.[27] That these attributes of Dutch republicanism are among those that especially attracted Smith appears from the following passage in Rae's *Life of Smith*:

> [Smith's] pupil and lifelong friend, the Earl of Buchan, says: "He approached to republicanism in his political principles, and considered a commonwealth as a platform for the monarchy, hereditary succession in the

21   Ibid., Bk. IV, Ch. II, p. 467.

22   Ibid., Bk. V, Ch. II, Pt. II, Art. IV, p. 906. The immense fiscal power of the Dutch was almost proverbial in the seventeenth and eighteenth centuries. Cf. Motley, *United Netherlands*, II, 74 n. and Jonathan Swift, *Examiner*, No. 13.

23   *Wealth of Nations*, Bk. I, Ch. IX, p. 111; Bk. III, Ch. IV, p. 424.

24   Ibid., Bk. IV, Ch. III, Pt. III, p. 613.

25   Ibid., Bk. V, Ch. III, p. 928.

26   Ibid., Bk. IV, Ch. III, Pt. II, p. 497.

27   *Federalist Paper*, No. 20.

chief magistrate being necessary only to prevent the commonwealth from being shaken by ambition, or absolute dominion introduced by the consequences of contending factions."[28]

It appears more authoritatively from Smith's own implicit expressions of his faith in the hereditary rather than the elective principle, for the practical reason that the qualities which would have to be discerned by electors are imperceptible by them, while the only qualities which the governed will venerate and hence obey easily are those automatically conferred by heredity.[29] It would be difficult to establish Smith's full view on the principle of hereditary monarchy from his own words, but fortunately it is not necessary to do this. We can establish that the executive was to be deprived of judicial functions,[30] and Smith's vigorous references to tyranny leave no doubt as to his general suspicion of the executive.[31] His conception of republicanism seems tantamount to constitutional monarchy qualified with separation of powers. Since the requirements of national survival caused Smith to take the side of indefinitely large states with indefinitely large populations, in the age-old controversy as to the optimum size of the political entity,[32] he also contemplates representative institutions as a matter of course. Representation is not to be according to population but according to the tax revenues taken from the representable jurisdictions.[33] Of the political qualifications of the laboring poor he wrote,

> But though the interest of the labourer is strictly con-
> nected with that of the society, he is incapable either of

---

28   John Rae, *Life of Adam Smith*, p. 124.

29   *Wealth of Nations*, Bk. III, Ch. II, p. 383–4; Bk. V, Ch. I, Pt. II, p. 713ff; *Theory of Moral Sentiments*, Pt. I, Sect. III, Ch. II, p. 52; Bk. VI, Sect. II, Ch. I, p. 226.

30   *Wealth of Nations*, Bk. V, Ch. I, Pt. III, p. 723.

31   Cf. e.g., ibid., Bk. V, Ch. I, Pt. III, Art. I, p. 729.

32   Consider Smith's concept of the progressive state of society: *Wealth of Nations*, Bk. I, Ch. VIII.

33   Ibid., Bk. IV, Ch. VII, Pt. III, pp. 622, 625; Bk. V, Ch. III, p. 933.

comprehending that interest, or of understanding its connexion with his own. His condition leaves him no time to receive the necessary information, and his education and habits are commonly such as to render him unfit to judge even though he was fully informed. In the public deliberations, therefore, his voice is little heard and less regarded, except upon some particular occasions, when his clamour is animated, set on, and supported by his employers, not for his, but their own particular purposes.[34]

He evidently did not mean to advance universal suffrage, or espouse democracy as we now understand it. The extent of his attachment to free polity, however is suggested by the passage wherein he declares in favor of standing armies:

That degree of liberty which approaches to licentious-ness can be tolerated only in countries where the sovereign is secured by a well-regulated standing army. It is in such countries only, that the public safety does not require, that the sovereign should be trusted with *any*[35] discretionary power for suppressing even the impertinent wantonness of this licentious liberty.[36]

Adam Smith's discussion of the distribution of authority in commercial society, although it does not form a distinct treatise, is inferentially handled in a significant way. A point on which Smith is most emphatic is that the mercantile class must not rule. That class comprises "an order of men, whose interest is never exactly the same with that of the public, who have generally an interest to deceive and even to oppress the public, and who accordingly have, upon many occasions, both deceived and oppressed it."[37] That interest moves "the mean rapacity and monopolizing spirit of merchants and manufacturers, who neither are, nor ought to be, the rulers of

---

34 Ibid., Bk. I, conc., p. 266; Bk. V, Ch. I, Pt. III, Art. II, pp. 781–3.

35 Italics not in original.

36 *Wealth of Nations*, Bk. V, Ch. I, Pt. I, p. 707.

37 Ibid., Bk. I, conc., p. 267.

mankind."[38] Concerning the administration of the East India Company,

> No other sovereigns ever were, or, from the nature of things, ever could be, so perfectly indifferent about the happiness or misery of their subjects, the improvement or waste of their dominions from irresistible moral causes, the greater part of the proprietors of such a mercantile company are, and necessarily must be.[39]

In general, "no two characters seem more inconsistent than those of trader and sovereign,"[40] not only because of the "irresistible moral causes" that affect mercantile dominion, but because the mass of mankind willingly obey only where they discern the marks of distinguished birth, or respectable lineage; whereas a government of

> merchants, a profession no doubt extremely respectable, . . . in no country in the world carries along with it that sort of authority which naturally overawes the people, and without force commands their willing obedience. Such a [governing] council can command obedience only by the military force with which they are accompanied, and their government is therefore necessarily military and despotical.[41]

No less certain is it that the government should not be engrossed into the hands of an hereditary nobility, for the concern of that order with the arts and appearances of rank must finally deprive them of the solid virtues of industry and application.[42] The hereditary nobility has the role, in Smithian soci-

---

38   Ibid., Bk. IV, Ch. III, Pt. II, p. 493.

39   Ibid., Bk. V, Ch. I, Pt. III, Art. II, p. 752.

40   Ibid., Bk. V, Ch. II, Pt. I, p. 819.

41   Ibid., Bk. IV, Ch. VII, Pt. III, p. 638. See also ibid., Bk. IV, Ch. VII, Pt. II, p. 570; Bk. IV, Ch. VII, Pt. III, p. 637; Bk. V, Ch. I, Pt. III, Art. I, pp. 737–8; Bk. V, Ch. II, Pt. II, Art. IV, p. 906.

42   *Theory of Moral Sentiments*, Pt. I, Sect. III, Ch. II, p. 55–6.

ety, of guaranteeing the general liberty by standing between the monarch and absolute power, on the premise that the real insignificance of the nobility is indispensable to, and an inevitable consequence of, tyrannical rule. Significantly, the very preoccupation with honor that traditional doctrine deemed desirable in public men is for Smith the ostensible ground for rejecting the aristocrats as rulers. "This exclusive privilege of the nobility to the great offices and honours of their country" is simply accounted the usurpation of an unjust advantage.[43]

Only for the completeness of the record need it be said that Smith rejected theocracy and absolute monarchy, i.e., the rule of the clergy or of a true sovereign prince.

Smith's political preference, so far as it is expressed, favors the "men who were educated in the middle and inferior ranks of life, who have been carried forward by their own industry and abilities,"[44] and are distinguished by the title of "natural aristocracy."[45] History abounds with the names of men of the type described by Smith, exemplified by an Englishman like Thomas Cromwell, and by Abraham Lincoln himself, as well as by the far more numerous class of public men stemming from the prosperous, respectable order of well-born common-ers; always, however, remembering the final indispensability of birth and wealth rather than excellence, to rule. The natural aristocracy seems to resemble a class of virtuous men such as would have been thought fit to bear rule by traditional stan-dards of polity; yet Smith does not place final reliance upon the virtue as such of the natural aristocracy; the stability and duration of free government depends "upon the power which the greater part of the leading men, the natural aristocracy of every country, have of preserving or defending their respec-tive importance."[46] The preservation of free polity depends upon the desire of these ambitious and high-spirited men to

---

43   *Wealth of Nations*, Bk. III, Ch. I, p. 385.

44   *Theory of Moral Sentiments*, Pt. I, Sect. III, Ch. II, p. 56.

45   *Wealth of Nations*, Bk. IV, Ch. VII, Pt. III, p. 622; Bk. V, Ch. I, Pt. I, p. 707.

46   Ibid., Bk. IV, Ch. VII, p. 622.

preserve their importance even at risk of life itself. Ultimately, their ambition and not their virtue is the support of the state, an idea which permeates the political speculation of our own early history.[47]

The theoretical foundation of this doctrine is in part to be found in the rejection of the idea of moral education, and the concomitant assertion of the full power of the passions over human life.[48] Not only are the citizens of the commercial society to be governed by the playing off of their passions against each other, but their governors are themselves to be governed similarly. Employing the usage of his age, Smith applies the term "management" to the process by which legislators are themselves guided.[49]

But further, this doctrine of polity depends in part upon a denial of the principle that only the better shall bear rule, or more precisely, that there exist a "best" fit to rule. In general, little may be expected of the virtue of the ruler himself, who is assumed by Smith to be of common understanding and distinguished by no moral superiority over any other rich man in the realm.[50]

It might be useful to summarize Smith's formulation of the political problem and its solution down to this point. Society is composed of orders, of which Smith identifies the

---

47   *Federalist Papers*, Nos. 10, 72, and 73; also Henry Clay, "Speech on the state of the country under Mr. Van Buren's administration" at Hanover Co., Va., June 27, 1840: "The pervading principle of our system of governments – of all free governments – is not merely the possibility, but the absolute certainty of infidelity and treachery, with even the highest functionary of the state; and hence all the restrictions, securities, and guarantees, which the wisdom of our ancestors or the sad experience of history had inculcated, have been devised and thrown around the chief magistrate." Cf. also Spinoza, *Political Treatise*, Ch. I, sec. 8.

48   See above, Ch. I, pp. 24 ff.

49   *Wealth of Nations*, Bk. IV, Ch. VII, Pt. III, pp. 622, 625. Eventually someone must attend to the question, Who will manage the managers?

50   Ibid., Bk. IV, Ch. IX, p. 687; Bk. V, Ch. III, pp. 908–9.

laboring poor, the landed gentry, merchants and manufacturers, the nobility, the clergy, and the sovereign himself. The political problem might be stated in the form, How shall the "powers, privileges, and immunities" of the several orders be assigned?[51] This formulation of the problem, as distinguished from Which order (or who) shall rule, is dictated by Smith's disqualification of each order for sole rule because its interests clash with those of the whole, i.e., because it is inherently unfit to bear rule. In other words, there is no conventional order qualified to bear rule. This is attested by Smith's reliance upon the "natural aristocracy," which is to say no order at all. Smith's affirmative solution is reliance upon a constitution which provides an arrangement or balancing of the orders, the arrangement as such taking the place of rule as such. The supreme importance of the constitutional arrangement is suggested by Smith's writing,

> [The successful politician] may re-establish and improve the constitution, and from the very doubtful and ambiguous character of the leader of a party, he may assume the *greatest and noblest of all characters*, that of the reformer and legislator of a great state; and by the wisdom of his institutions, secure the internal tranquility and happiness of his fellow-citizens for many succeeding generations.[52]

* * *

We have yet to consider the largest meaning of the freedom which is both root and flower of liberal commercial society – the freedom of the individual from the restraint of implausible, seemingly unattainable virtue as such, and his release into the custody of his own natural impulses. Smith has made nothing plainer than his belief that social life is dominated by

---

51 See *Theory of Moral Sentiments*, Pt. VI, Sect. II, Ch. II, p. 230 ff.

52 Ibid., Pt. VI, Sect. II, Ch. II, p. 232. Italics not in original. It is noteworthy that Smith assumes the legislator to be self-taught, i.e., not taught by philosophers.

"the uniform, constant, and uninterrupted effort of every man to better his condition"[53] with the understanding that "an augmentation of fortune is the means by which the greater part of men propose and wish to better their condition." At the same time "it is the means the most vulgar and the most obvious."[54] Desirable society is that in which this effort is

> . . . protected by law and allowed by liberty to exert itself in the manner that is most advantageous. . . . It is the highest impertinence and presumption, therefore, in kings and ministers, to pretend to watch over the æconomy of private people, and to restrain their expence, either by sumptuary laws, or by prohibiting the importation of foreign luxuries. They are themselves always, and without any exception, the greatest spendthrifts in the society. Let them look well after their own expence, and they may safely trust private people with theirs. If their own extravagance does not ruin the state, that of their subjects never will.[55]

Having stated this, Adam Smith has argued that commercial society rests upon polity that emancipates men from liberality and temperance, or more precisely, raises from their spirits the fearful inhibitions that are required to restrain their desires and their advantage at once. Liberalism is the social form which is in the first instance clear of the tyrannical power of the censor, and in the second instance least likely to foster the growth of that power; for where men literally govern themselves they can easily fend off the laws that bind them, even the laws that confine them to liberality, temperance, and similar salutary habits. The direct relation between free polity and the crucial passion to better one's condition explains better than any other principle could, why Smith constructed his system upon that passion and not upon the famous fear of violent death that supports the system of his great antecessor. The

---

53 *Wealth of Nations*, Bk. II, Ch. III, p. 346; also Bk. II, Ch. III, pp. 341, 345; Bk. IV, Ch. V, p. 540; Bk. IV, Ch. IX, p. 674.

54 Ibid., Bk. II, Ch. III, p. 341–2.

55 Ibid., Bk. II, Ch. III, p. 345–6.

desire of bettering one's condition is the endless impulse always to add to the means of preservation, and it depends essentially upon free use of powers. The desire to forestall violence may be satisfied by the effective restraint of all others, and it depends essentially upon a privation of the free use of powers. The freedom implicit in the Smithian principle is accompanied by restraint, and the authoritative restraint implicit in the Hobbean formula is the necessary condition of freedom, but in sum, Smith's principle was intended to, and did, lead to liberal society, while that of Hobbes need not have done so. We might go so far as to say that it was by the substitution of the desire to better one's condition for the fear of violent death as the critical passion of man, that Smith accomplished both the liberalization and commercialization of the Hobbean system.

We see hereby the sense in which it is true that free and commercial society must be coeval. "Freedom" is a discharge from the inhibitions that traditionally were known as virtues. For these latter are substituted the controlled passions of self-preservation through gain, the unhampered motion of which is commerce.[56] The crucial importance of free competition in commercial society springs from the fact that competition is the element in commercialism that directly replaces virtue. Competition rather than the artificial regulations of gild and state is to guarantee probity in manufacture and sale,[57] and it is competition rather than legislation that shall provide the right norm of prices, which norm is the natural price, as distinguished from the "just price" of earlier centuries. It is for a

---

56 Perhaps the most forthright statement of the replacement of virtue by commerce is given by Montesquieu, *Spirit of Laws*, III, iii: "The Greek political writers, who lived under free government, did not recognize any force which could uphold them but that of virtue. Those of today speak to us only of manufactures, commerce, finance, wealth, and even of luxury." Rousseau's expression is similar: "The ancient politicians spoke incessantly of morals and virtue; ours speak only of commerce and money." (*Discourse on the Arts and Sciences*).

57 *Wealth of Nations*, Bk. I *passim*.

good reason, as we shall see presently, that Smith refers to the natural price as "the price of free competition."[58] It is this substitution of competition for virtue that we must try to understand more fully, and at the same time attempt to discover Smith's judgment on the substitution.

* * *

Smith begins his discussion of the natural price of commodities with some remarks on the natural rates of wages, profits, and rent, a commencement which accords with our general understanding that there is a profound relation between the problem of value and the problem of distribution. Smith writes,

> There is in every society or neighbourhood an ordinary or average rate both of wages and profit in every different employment of labour and stock. . . . There is likewise in every society or neighbourhood an ordinary or average rate of rent. . . . These ordinary or average rates may be called the natural rates of wages, profit, and rent, *at the time and place in which they commonly prevail.*[59]

We learn first of all that the natural rates of wages, profit, and rent are the ordinary or average rates common to particular societies or neighborhoods, or that each pertains to the particular time and place in which it prevails. That such temporal and local norms should be titled natural, although the natural is thought to be everywhere and at all times the same, is a striking fact to which we shall turn later. At present, however, we must note the relation of the natural rates to the natural price:

> When the price of any commodity is neither more nor less than what is sufficient to pay the rent of the land, the wages of the labour, and the profit of the stock

---

58   Ibid., Bk. I, Ch. VII, p. 78.
59   Ibid., Bk. I, Ch. VII, p. 72. Italics not in original.

employed in raising, preparing, and bringing it to
market, according to their natural rates, the commodity is then sold for what may be called its natural
price.[60]

The first fact that we have concerning the natural price is
derivative from facts concerning the natural rates of compen-
sation to the factors of production: the natural price is the sum
of the distributive shares when those are at their natural rates.
What then are those distributive shares, and what is it that
governs them, in turn, and their "natural rates?"

The distributive shares are portions of the value of a commodity assigned to various recipients for two sets of reasons,
one exemplified by wages, the other by profits and rents.
Wages are the portion of the value of a commodity which is
assigned to labor. The source of the value of things is, according to Smith, labor. Labor seems to acquire its distributive
share in virtue of its capacity as source of value, on the unstat-
ed premise that to labor upon something is to acquire rights of
ownership over it. Thus in the early and rude, or pre-civilized
state of society, wherein the only productive resource which is
owned is labor, "the whole produce of labour belongs to the
laborer."[61] However, when capital accumulates, i.e., when
some men come to possess stocks of goods which can be used
in the process of production; then, writes Smith, "[the master]
shares in the produce of [the workmen's] labour, or in the
value which it adds to the materials upon which it is
bestowed; and in this share consists his profit."[62] Likewise, "as
soon as land becomes private property, the landlord demands
a share of almost all the produce which the labourer can either
raise, or collect from it. His rent makes the first deduction from
the produce of the labour which is employed upon land."[63]
Smith's account of profit and rent is remarkable, and quite
explicit. After the accumulation of stock, "[t]he value which

---

60   Ibid., Bk. I, Ch. VII, p. 72.
61   Ibid., Bk. I, Ch. VI, p. 65.
62   Ibid., Bk. I, Ch. VIII, p. 83.
63   Ibid., Bk. I, Ch. VIII, p. 83.

the workmen add to the materials, therefore, resolves itself . . . into two parts, of which the one pays their wages, the other the profits of their employer."[64] Rent is simply the result of the further resolution of the value added by labor, according to Smith.[65] According to this well-known analysis of Smith's, therefore, wages are a distributive share going to labor in virtue of its capacity as the source of value, and profit and rent are distributive shares going to the owners of capital and land in virtue of their conventional or legal right to share in the value of things created through labor with or upon their property.

But how will the distribution be made between workmen and masters, and between farmers and landlords? What governs the process of "resolution?" From Smith's point of view, the answer was not obscure, following as it does directly from the conventional character of the distributive shares themselves. "What are the common wages of labour, depends every where upon the contract usually made between [the masters and workmen]."[66] Also, rent "considered as the price paid for the use of the land" (that is, considered as a distributive share rather than as a theoretical differential determined at the margin of cultivation) "is naturally a monopoly price. It is not at all proportioned to what the landlord may have laid out upon the improvement of the land, or to what he can afford to take; but to what the farmer can afford to give."[67] In simple language, Smith's position is that the distribution of value in a civilized, or commercial society is determined by the bargaining power of the parties to the wage and rent contracts. We must not forget that it is in his chapter on wages that Smith describes the effects of combination on bargaining power – combination on the part of masters and workmen alike for the sake of affecting the distribution of value between them.

---

64 Ibid., Bk. I, Ch. VI, p. 66.
65 Ibid., Bk. I, Ch. VI, pp. 67–8.
66 Ibid., Bk. I, Ch. VIII, p. 83.
67 Ibid., Bk. I, Ch. XI, p. 161. Also, "every landlord acting the part of a monopolist," etc., ibid., Bk. I, Ch. X, Pt. II, p. 134.

Our inference from Smith's writing is that wages, profit, and rent are by their nature conventional, based upon contract in the most literal and exclusive sense in that the shares themselves arise through convention or contract and in that the *rates* of wages, profit, and rent are the issue of transitory agreements or contracts. The conventional is opposed to the natural; yet Smith repeatedly speaks of the natural rates of wages, profit, and rent. In what sense can the distributive shares be conceived as "natural?"

In the case of wages and profit, the "rate is naturally regulated . . . partly by the general circumstances of the society, their riches or poverty, their advancing, stationary, or declining condition; and partly by the particular nature of each employment."[68] The case of rent is similar in that it too is regulated "partly by the general circumstances of the society or neighbourhood in which the land is situated, and partly by the natural or improved fertility of the land."[69] But "the particular nature of each employment" and the "natural or improved fertility of the land" account only for the inequality of the natural rates of wages, profit, and rent in different employments, i.e., for the relation among the natural rates; they do not account for the determination of the absolute level of those natural rates. For that we must look to "the general circumstances of the society or neighbourhood."

At any time, each society is either advancing, stationary, or declining in its wealth. If it is stationary, it has attained its "full complement of riches,"[70] which full complement is a function of the nation's laws and institutions, and its soil, climate, and geographical situation.[71] The soil, climate, and situation are truly the nation's "natural" endowment, but they are not decisive for the progress of the country, since with better institutions, any society but the absolutely perfect one can be imagined capable of progress. In the advancing society, the

---

68   Ibid., Bk. I, Ch. VII, p. 72.

69   Ibid.

70   Ibid., Bk. I, Ch. VIII, p. 99; Bk. I, Ch. IX, pp. 110, 111, 112.

71   Ibid., Bk. I, Ch. IX, p. 111–2.

natural rate of wages will be high, the natural rate of profits low, and the natural rate of rent high. In the retrograde society, the natural rate of wages will fall to less than the subsistence level, (i.e., the population will decrease),[72] the natural rate of profit will rise, and that of rent decline. This is, of course, perfectly well known. Equally well known, perhaps, is the fact that the progress, stagnation, or retrogression of society works its effects upon the natural rates through the force of competition exclusively. To take an example, the progress of society would witness an increase in stock and an increased demand for labor, with laborers being put at a temporary bargaining advantage and masters bidding up their wages. The outcome is everywhere determined by the competitive contract of the bargainers, and the distinction between progressive, stationary, and declining states simply expresses the fact that the general situation will sometimes favor one party to the contract and sometimes another. The natural rate literally defines the norm towards which, *at any time and place*, the actual rates will tend to gravitate; no more. There is no substantive natural principle to which the natural rates must conform, only the formal principle that the effectual demand for, and the supply of the productive facility will be equated at the natural rate. A substantive principle would be, for example, that the natural rate of wages or profit shall be just sufficient to allow a man to bequeath to his children as much as he inherited; or to enable every man to live in, and to depart life from, the station into which he was born. The absence of any substantive norm in Smith's description of the "natural" is proved by the fact that it could not even be translated into the premise that the natural rate must be at least sufficient to preserve life. It need not be. It can fall below the subsistence level, and it can include very considerable convenience, perhaps luxury, even for the wage earner. Whether it does the one or the other

---

72 Ibid., Bk. I, Ch. VIII, p. 91: "Want, famine, and mortality would immediately prevail in [the lowest] class, and from thence extend themselves to all the superior classes, till the number of inhabitants in the country was reduced to what could easily be maintained by the revenue and stock which remained in it," etc.

depends upon the contract or convention which comes to subsist between the seller and the buyer of the factor of production. Smith's natural rates of wages, profit, and rent clearly are not natural in the sense of coinciding with or having an internal congruence with man's nature; for they are compatible with his destruction and with the destruction or abasement of his nature. They are not natural in the sense of being supraconventional. In what sense then are they natural?[73]

We must recur to Smith's conception of the natural. We know that the word "natural" for Smith carries with it the idea of conflict with the perfectly virtuous. It is in "the natural course of things" that "a great combination of men should prevail over a small one," a rule that sometimes has as its consequence that "violence and artifice prevail over sincerity and justice."[74] But this very fact of combination, or most generally, of power in the sense of bargaining power, assumes a large importance in Smith's discussion of the apportionment of distributive shares. He writes,

> What are the common wages of labour, depends every where upon the contract made between workmen and masters, whose interests are by no means the same. The workmen desire to get as much, the masters to give as little as possible. The former are disposed to combine in order to raise, the latter in order to lower the wages of labour.

---

73   The position that Smith's "natural wage" is not really natural in that it contains no substantive normal principle might be criticized as overlooking the fact that the natural wage cannot indefinitely remain below the subsistence level; i.e., the society cannot retrogress indefinitely. The natural wage will eventually be restored at least to the level of bare subsistence. But the truth of this does not imply the equivalence of the natural wage and the subsistence wage, i.e., the substantive character of the natural wage. What is meant is rather that the natural wage, over great lengths of time, has about the same relation to the subsistence wage as in shorter periods the market price has to the natural price. Nothing about this, I believe, suggests the normative or substantive character of the natural wage itself.

74   *Theory of Moral Sentiments*, Pt. III, Ch. V, pp. 168–9.

> It is not, however, difficult to foresee which of the two
> parties must, upon all ordinary occasions, have the
> advantage in the dispute, and force the other into a
> compliance with their terms.[75]

Nor can it be said that such combination would not exist
under the free competition characteristic of the natural order.
In a famous passage, Smith wrote,

> People of the same trade seldom meet together, even
> for merriment and diversion, but the conversation
> ends in a conspiracy against the public, or in some
> contrivance to raise prices. It is impossible indeed to
> prevent such meetings, by any law which either could
> be executed, or would be consistent with liberty and
> justice.[76]

Such meetings and their sequels would therefore not be absent
from the competitive system as Smith conceived it.

Smith's definition of rent as "naturally a monopoly price"
dependent not upon what the landlord can afford to take but
what the farmer can afford to give[77] clearly reflects his belief
that agrarian shares are determined according to substantially
the same formula of relative bargaining powers as governs
wages and profit.

The view that each man shall appropriate or make his own
as much as his power enables him to do is neither original
with Smith nor decisive in itself, since it is possible and indeed
necessary to go beyond the mere expression of the fact, if it is
a fact, and to judge of its desirability as a principle of action.
In a famous passage of a work which is a classic for modern
social science, Spinoza wrote,

---

75 *Wealth of Nations*, Pt. I, Ch. VIII, p. 83. We now perceive that it is
    more difficult than Smith knew it to be, to foresee which party
    would prevail; but our interest is not in the outcome as much as
    in Smith's conception of the process by which the distributive
    shares are apportioned.

76 Ibid., Bk. I, Ch. X, Pt. II, p. 145.

77 Ibid., Bk. I, Ch. XI, p. 161.

And so by natural right I understand the very laws or
rules of nature, in accordance with which everything
takes place, in other words, the power of nature itself.
And so the natural right of universal nature, and consequently of every individual thing, extends as far as
its power; and accordingly, whatever any man does
after the laws of his nature, he does by the highest natural right, and he has as much right over nature as he
has power.[78]

So writing, Spinoza affirmed the identity of the full exercise of
power (by which he meant power to preserve one's existence)
with the naturally *right*: or more precisely, that there is no such
thing as the naturally right apart from the full exercise of powers, which comprise each man's rights by nature. Whereas
Smith's argument implies the correspondence of the requirements of nature and preservation on the one hand with the full
exercise of powers on the other, he does distinguish the natural from the right or just, conceiving that the practical deci-
siveness of power is indeed natural but that it is compatible
with the victory of violence and artifice over sincerity and justice; with the success of knaves, albeit industrious;[79] i.e., with
the opposite of the right. The presence of this vestige of traditional morality in Smith, in the form of a radical distinction
between the self-preservative, even though "natural," and the
just, raises a profound question as to the reasons for Smith's
final advocacy of the system of competitive commerce.
Postponing the question for treatment in Chapter III below, let
us here suggest a hypothesis by quoting again for careful
examination by the reader, an often-cited remark of Smith's
"intimate and valued friend" Millar:

> In the last part of his lectures, he examined those polit-
> ical regulations which are founded, not upon the prin-
> ciple of justice, but that of expediency, and which are
> calculated to increase the riches, the power, and the
> prosperity of a State. Under this view, he considered

78 *Political Treatise*, Ch. II, sec. 4, tr. Elwes.
79 *Theory of Moral Sentiments*, Pt. III, Ch. V, pp. 168–9.

the political institutions relating to commerce, to finances, to ecclesiastical and military establishments. What he delivered on these subjects contained the substance of the work he afterwards published under the title of *An Inquiry into the Nature and Causes of the Wealth of Nations.*[80]

Our most general conclusion from the foregoing, at least until we examine Smith's intention in the widest sense, is that freedom, conceived as liberation from onerous restraints in behalf of virtue, may be sought through the competitive commercial ordering of society, and indeed can only be sought thereby.

Our view of essential commercial society would be incomplete if it overlooked the fact that it is not only, or perhaps not even primarily, the civil government that trammels the people with sumptuary laws, rules of just price, usury enactments, and many other infinitely more comprehensive commandments, but rather the spiritual government of the clergy. We cannot forget that it was casuistry, or the ecclesiastical system of morality, that sought to orient human conduct upon man's duties, and that Smith not only excluded benevolence from the calendar of political virtues, but also rejected casuistry and duties alike in favor of jurisprudence, mere justice, and rights.[81] With such a theoretical preparation, Smith is simply being consistent when he views the natural order of life as essentially secular; freedom in the present context means a privation of the inhibitions that proceed not only from the civil but also from the ecclesiastical authority. Both authorities, when they attempt to compress human life within the strait limits of virtue, deny the vital needs and hence the sovereign passions of man and must be dispensed with as against nature. If, however, we wish to know the ultimate sources of Smith's rejection of ecclesiastical society, we cannot rest content with his merely theoretical reasonings. He advances such strong and persistent objections to clerical authority on

---

80 Quoted by Dugald Stewart in his biographical remarks upon Smith, published as a preface to the 1795 edition of Smith's essays, p. xviii.

81 Above, Ch. I, pp. 33 ff.

grounds of political convenience, that we are bound to reflect whether those theoretical reasonings are the whole inspiration, or only the *a priori* vindication of his entire program respecting religion.

We observe first a great ground of conflict between unconfined religion and civil freedom:

> When the authorized teachers of religion propagate through the great body of the people doctrines subversive of the authority of the sovereign, it is by violence only, or by the force of a standing army, that he can maintain his authority.[82]

No polity except a secularized one can upon these terms remain free. In the same vein, but more generally, it is argued that the clergy form an order which, by its power over the people's minds and its capacity for supplanting fear of the sovereign with a larger terror managed by themselves, is a perpetual menace to the good order of society.[83] The greater the influence of the clergy, the greater the danger to the legitimate fruits of society; and the greatest danger accompanies the greatest influence:

> In the state in which things were through the greater part of Europe during the tenth, eleventh, twelfth, and thirteenth centuries, and for some time both before and after that period, the constitution of the church of Rome may be considered as the most formidable combination that ever was formed against the authority and security of civil government, as well as against the liberty, reason, and happiness of mankind, which can flourish only where civil government is able to protect them.[84]

The violent dominion of what Smith unfailingly condemns as superstition[85] is what he is supremely anxious to banish from

82   *Wealth of Nations*, Bk. V, Ch. I, Pt. III, Art. III, pp. 797–8.
83   Ibid., Bk. V, Ch. I, Pt. III, Art. III, pp. 792–3, 796–8, 802, 805–6.
84   Ibid., Bk. V, Ch. I, Pt. III, Art. III, p. 803.
85   Ibid., Bk. V, Ch. I, Pt. III, Art. III, pp. 793, 796, 803.

society, a fact that we may overlook only at the price of never fully understanding the reasons for Smith's advocacy of commercial society.

The secular disposition of the natural order is well attested in Article III, Chapter I, Book V of the *Wealth of Nations*, wherein are considered the religious institutions of commercial society. In the first place, religion is discussed as a collection of "Institutions for the Instruction of People of all Ages," the idea of worship and of Divinity being absent from title and discourse alike. By this it is not meant to suggest that commercial society is conceived by Smith as irreligious; on the contrary, religions would abound. The sign of the role of religion in free commercial society is given by Smith's intimation that under the best circumstances, the community would be divided into perhaps two or three thousand small sects, each too petty "to disturb the public tranquility."[86] It goes without saying that Smith could not have desired even two to exist if he had believed in the verity of either, so that we may safely put doctrinal rectitude aside as irrelevant to his stand on divinity. However, the "great multitude" of sects would eventually "reduce the doctrine of the greater part of them to that pure and rational religion, free from every mixture of absurdity, imposture, or fanaticism, such as wise men have in all ages of the world wished to see established."[87] The principle of divide and conquer is as well illustrated herein as anywhere. And most providentially, not only would the multitude of sects neutralize the menace of the clergy against the order of society, but the very number and pettiness of the sects would solve the difficult problem of disciplining the great turbulent urban populations inseparable from commercial society. In small communities, the citizens' conduct is regulated by their constant mutual surveillance; in great cities, the universal anonymity of the mass shakes the foundation of good behavior. Each man's membership in a small sect will in effect incorporate him in a small community and submit him again to that detailed scrutiny by his fellows which will fortify him against

---

86   Ibid., Bk. V, Ch. I, Pt. III, Art. III, p. 793.
87   Ibid.

evil. It is to be distinctly observed that the moral effect of religion is produced not exclusively or principally through any anticipation of reward or punishment to be visited upon the immortal soul but through the mutual supervision that prevails in small religious communities as small communities, and not as religions. In this we see the full force of secularism in full presence of religion.[88]

Under certain unfavorable circumstances, viz., where politics had "called in the aid of religion,"[89] the establishment of a single sect to be the official religion of the realm was inevitable. So would it always be. In spite of Hume's unabashed argument in favor of establishment, quoted by Smith *in extenso,* Smith himself inclines against establishment; for the multitude of sects would conduce to the pure and rational religion which "positive law has perhaps never yet established, and probably never will establish in any country: because, with regard to religion, positive law always has been, and probably always will be, more or less influenced by popular superstition and enthusiasm."[90] However, should the nation find itself with an established church, the cause of the sovereign is not yet lost:

> [For] though this order of men [the clergy] can scarce
> ever be forced, they may be managed as easily as any
> other; and the security of the sovereign, as well as the
> public tranquillity, seems to depend very much upon
> the means which he has of managing them; and those

---

88 Ibid., Bk. V, Ch. I, Pt. III, Art. III, p. 794–5. It is unnecessary to point out that Smith elected in favor of large societies rather than small because of the superior viability of the former. Yet he is obliged in one way or another to acknowledge and provide against the moral disadvantages of mass society by simulating the conditions of small republics. Those who concentrated their attention upon the moral disadvantages of mass societies found in favor of the small; those who concentrated upon viability found in favor of the large.

89 Ibid., Bk. V, Ch. I, Pt. III, Art. III, p. 792.

90 Ibid., Bk. V, Ch. I, Pt. III, Art. III, p. 793.

means seem to consist altogether in the preferment which he has to bestow upon them.[91]

The remainder of Smith's writing on the subject concerns the techniques for taking advantage of the fact that the clergy, like all other orders of men, are ruled by their interest and their necessities, both of which are prescribed to them by nature in the way familiar to us.

Smith plainly treats of religion in the manner of a man handling a substance which in proper amounts is a benignant medicine but of which a large draft is toxic. His plan for society must be accounted secular, not in that it dispenses with religion (any more than did the systems of those other philosophers who wrote approvingly of rational religion) but in that it contemplates "pure and rational" religion, free of "enthusiasm and superstition" or, in fine, mitigated, neutralized and synthetic religion entirely in the service of public morality. In effect Smith has proposed to himself the question, How may society procure the moral advantages of religion without its civil and other inconveniences? His answer must be considered as given under two categories, the first being, as we have seen, religion under the form of a multiplicity of puny sects; and the second, as we shall see, religion offset by a judicious combination of "education" and "poetry."

Smith's treatise on academic or "literary" education[92] may for our present purpose be considered as divided into two parts, one concerning universities and the education of "people of some rank and fortune," the other concerning the education of the mass of the people. Smith reproved the universities of his day as the fountainheads of the unconfirmed subtleties (eventuating in "cobweb science") that constitute a preparation for life in another world; in general, "philosophy was taught only as subservient to theology."[93] But the proper role of universities is "the education of gentlemen or men of

91 Ibid., Bk. V, Ch. I, Pt. III, Art. III, p. 799.

92 Ibid., Bk. V, Ch. I, Pt. III, Art. II; distinguished from the subsequent article, which concerns education through religious means.

93 Ibid., Bk. V, Ch. I, Pt. III, Art. II, p. 770.

the world."[94] in order to prepare them for "the real business of the world."[95] When the universities are rightly ordered, they will revert to the ancient principle of teaching in three completely terrestrial divisions – natural philosophy, logic, and moral philosophy, of which the last, "by far the most important of all the different branches of philosophy,"[96] will be purged of casuistry,

> a debased system of moral philosophy, which was considered as immediately connected with the doctrines of Pneumatology, with the immortality of the human soul, and with the rewards and punishments which, from the justice of the Deity, were to be expected in a life to come.[97]

We need no longer labor the point that the universities are intended by Smith to be the free[98] sources of specifically humane or secular learning. The immense importance of the universities depends upon the fact that their influence by far transcends the men who pass through them in person; it literally permeates society. For "science is the great antidote to the poison of enthusiasm and superstition; and where all the superior ranks of people were secured from it, *the inferior ranks could not be much exposed to it.*"[99]

But what is the place in this structure of the inferior ranks of the populace? We learn that upon their freedom from "enthusiasm and superstition" depend the liberty and good

---

94 Ibid., Bk. V, Ch. I, Pt. III, Art. II, pp. 772–3, 781.

95 Ibid., Bk. V, Ch. I, Pt. III, Art. II, p. 773. Thus the radical view that the schools should abandon their traditional role of disseminators of theoretical wisdom to the few is associated with the intention to secularize them along with society at large.

96 Ibid., Bk. V, Ch. I, Pt. III, Art. II, p. 771.

97 Ibid., Bk. V, Ch. I, Pt. III, Art. II, p. 772.

98 Not subject to any "extraneous jurisdiction . . . liable to be exercised both ignorantly and capriciously. In its nature (such an authority) is arbitrary and discretionary," etc. ibid., Bk. V, Ch. I, Pt. III, Art. II, p. 761.

99 Ibid., Bk. V, Ch. I, Pt. III, Art. III, p. 796. Italics not in original.

order of society; that the populace must be instructed until they are proof against "the delusions of enthusiasm and superstition, which, among ignorant nations, frequently occasion the most dreadful disorders;"[100] and that "in free countries, where the safety of government depends very much upon the favorable judgment which the people may form of its conduct, it must surely be of the highest importance that they should not be disposed to judge rashly or capriciously concerning it."[101]

As regards the great body of the people, it is unnecessary to reproduce the details of the argument, for we need know only the general principle that the government of commercial society must "rationalize" the populace, i.e., provide the people with the maximum of "literary education" which they can absorb, for the reasons already made plain.[102]

Smith offers a second expedient for counteracting the public effects of such "enthusiasm and superstition" as would grow from the multitude of sects. The remedy is "the frequency and gaiety of public diversions."[103] From the point of view

---

100 Ibid., Bk. V, Ch. I, Pt. III, Art. II, p. 788.

101 Ibid., Bk. V, Ch. I, Pt. III, Art. II, p. 788. As an evidence of Smith's descent from Hobbes, the following passage from *Leviathan*, Review and Conclusion (Molesworth, p. 713) is given in full: "For seeing the Universities are the fountains of civil and moral doctrine, from whence the preachers, and the gentry, drawing such water as they find, use to sprinkle the same (both from the pulpit and in their conversation), upon the people, there ought certainly to be great care taken, to have it pure, both from the venom of heathen politicians, and from the incantation of deceiving spirits. And by that means the most men, knowing their duties, will be the less subject to serve the ambition of a few discontented persons, in their purposes against the state; and be the less grieved with the contribution necessary for their peace, and defence; and the governors themselves have the less cause, to maintain at the common charge any greater army, than is necessary to make good the public liberty, against the invasions and encroachments of foreign enemies."

102 *Wealth of Nations*, Bk. V, Ch. I, Pt. III, Art. II, pp. 784 ff.

103 Ibid., Bk. V, Ch. I, Pt. III, Art. II, p. 796.

of the present age, there is nothing provocative of controversy or even of great interest in the proposal to mollify the austerity of manners with "painting, poetry, music, dancing, and all sorts of dramatic representations." Yet the eighteenth century knew this matter as a subject of philosophic debate, exemplified by d'Alembert's *Encyclopedia* article on Geneva taxing that city for its expulsion of the theater, and Rousseau's famous rejoinder, the "Lettre à d'Alembert sur les spectacles." Rousseau defended the Genevan anti-theatrical policy as being best suited to the life of a small republic founded upon virtue and religion. Smith addressed himself to the requirements of a large republic founded upon commerce. He therefore believed himself required to stipulate for the "humanization" of society. One area of humanization is the stage; others, more important, are the schools themselves.

We have come now to perceive commercial society in terms of its two decisive characteristics: civil and ecclesiastical freedom, or, in other words, liberty and secularism. The boldness of the design that joins these two elements together is best appreciated in its contrast with earlier conceptions. Before Smith's epoch, it was a settled principle of political life, and philosophy that fear of the prince and fear of power invisible were alike indispensable to common life. Not for its subtlety but rather for its simplicity. The expression of the Tudor statesman Sir William Paget may serve as the type of this precept: "Society in a realm doth consist and is maintained by means of religion and law, and these two or one wanting, farewell all just society, government, justice."[104] This view was neither obscure nor obviously contemptible, and it required to be met in one way or another. What was Smith's answer to the fundamental question, How can good order be had in the absence of strong secular or oppressive ecclesiastical restraints

---

104 Quoted in Froude, *History of England*, vol. V, p. 121. The doctrine was so firmly established that it might even account for the adherence of philosophers to the ecclesiastical principle of society until it cost them their lives. Consider the events of the reign of Henry VIII.

upon the people? The answer may be summarized in this formula: through the dilution of ecclesiastical authority by means available to a society unencumbered with enthusiasm and superstition, viz., humanized, civilized, commercial society.[105]

We see that Smith had not merely sought to provide an answer to the argument that society is impossible without authoritative collaboration by civil and ecclesiastical governors; he had sought to invert that argument into the form: liberal, humane society requires to be rid of authoritative rule by civil governors, which it can accomplish only by ridding itself at the same time of authoritative ecclesiastical government. The revolution was accomplished by turning to practical account a moral theory that announced the entire primacy of the passions over reason; the derivation of the politically defensible and desirable from the identification of nature with preservation; the subversion of proud superiority to gain; and the principle of the equality of all human beings in their paramount right to preservation of life. The utilization of the theory took the form of a plan for society based upon the desire of each member to pursue the pleasure of gain without end, or in other words, the plan of commercial society. The grand design in behalf of free society, requiring the emancipation from the reign of virtue that commerce makes possible, relied heavily upon the power of education successfully to humanize and "rationalize" the entire population. Through such literary

---

105 Here especially it should be recalled that Smith identified commercial and civilized society (see below pp. 111), and like Montesquieu (*Spirit of Laws*, XX, 1–2) affirmed the humanizing effects of commerce, the means of "that mutual communication of knowledge and of all sorts of improvements;" (*Wealth of Nations*, Bk. IV, Ch. VII, Pt. III, p. 627) and "which ought naturally to be, among nations, as among individuals, a bond of union and friendship" (Ibid., Bk. IV, Ch. III, Pt. II, p. 493; Bk. III, Ch. III, p. 406; Bk. III, Ch. IV, pp. 412–3, 417, 421–2; Bk. V, Ch. I, Pt. II, p. 711; Bk. V, Ch. I, Pt. III, Art. 3d, p. 803). Commerce is humanizing in the sense of promoting peace through familiarity with others and their ways, not of fostering benevolence.

education as they might support, the masses would be inspired to the temperate judgment and mildness of manners that alone can tolerate the responsibilities of freedom so understood.[106]

---

106 It is not inappropriate to conclude this chapter with the words in which Motley described the spirit of Holland and, implicitly, of all commercial societies. Of the States-General he wrote: "Nevertheless these men believed that they understood the spirit of their country and of the age. In encouragement to an expanding commerce, the elevation and education of the masses, the toleration of all creeds, and a wide distribution of political functions and rights, they looked for the salvation of their nascent republic from destruction, and the maintenance of the true interests of the people." *United Netherlands*, Vol. II, Ch. XII, p. 127.

CHAPTER III
THE PROBLEM OF SMITH'S INTENTION

Adam Smith is properly famous as the great expositor and advocate of the principle of free commercial society, or what we now speak of as capitalism; so much so that his name has passed into a byword, signifying liberalism. And yet there is contained in the interstices of his exposition such a critique of the system advocated as must raise in our minds the deepest questions as to the nature and meaning of his advocacy. Smith's animadversions upon some aspects of commercialism have been noticed often enough,[1] but they have too commonly been passed over without adequate explanation. In this chapter we shall attempt to account for their presence by reconciling them with the most general aspects of Smith's teaching.

We have first to notice that Smith deprecated the elementary moral basis itself of commercial society and marked it as inferior to what he conceived to be its major alternative. Thus in the abstract, the principle of benevolence is without qualification preferable to the principle of mercantile justice.[2] This

---

1   See for example Prof. Cannan's introduction to *Wealth of Nations*, pp. xxxiii–xxxiv (Modern Library, New York, 1937).

2   "All the members of human society stand in need of each other's assistance, and are likewise exposed to mutual injuries. Where the necessary assistance is reciprocally afforded from love, from gratitude, from friendship, and esteem, the society flourishes and is happy. All the different members of it are bound together by the agreeable bands of love and affection, and are, as it were, thereby drawn to one common centre of mutual good offices.

matter was treated in Chapter I above, where the theoretical origin of the position was traced to Smith's doctrines of nature.

In the second place, passing from the basis of commercial society to its effects upon the quality of life, we perceive a variety of critical observations. Perhaps the most striking have to do with the moral and intellectual deterioration of the laboring poor in a society founded upon the thoroughgoing division of labor, i.e., commercial society. Thus,

> In the progress of the division of labour, the employment of the far greater part of those who live by labour, that is, of the great body of the people, comes to be confined to a few very simple operations, frequently to one or two. But the understandings of the greater part of men are necessarily formed by their ordinary employments. The man whose whole life is spent in performing a few simple operations, of which the effects too are, perhaps, always the same, or very nearly the same, has no occasion to exert his understanding, or to exercise his invention in finding out expedients for removing difficulties which never occur. He naturally loses, therefore, the habit of such exertion, and generally becomes as stupid and ignorant as it is possible for a human creature to become. The torpor of his mind renders him, not only incapable of relishing or bearing a part in any rational conversation, but of conceiving any generous, noble, or

---

But though the necessary assistance should not be afforded from such generous and disinterested motives, though among the different members of the society there should be no mutual love and affection, the society, though less happy and agreeable, will not necessarily be dissolved. Society may subsist, among different men, as among different merchants, from a sense of its utility, without any mutual love or affection; and though no man in it should owe any obligation, or be bound in gratitude to any other, it may still be upheld by a mercenary exchange of good offices according to an agreed valuation." *Theory of Moral Sentiments*, Pt. II, Sect. II, Ch. III, pp. 85–6.

tender sentiment, and consequently of forming any just judgment concerning many even of the ordinary duties of private life. Of the great and extensive interests of his country he is altogether incapable of judging; and unless very particular pains have been taken to render him otherwise, he is equally incapable of defending his country in war. The uniformity of his stationary life naturally corrupts the courage of his mind, and makes him regard with abhorrence the irregular, uncertain, and adventurous life of a soldier. It corrupts even the activity of his body, and renders him incapable of exerting his strength with vigor and perseverance, in any other employment than that to which he has been bred. His dexterity at his own particular trade seems, in this manner, to be acquired at the expence of his intellectual, social, and martial virtues. But in every improved and civilized society this is the state into which the labouring poor, that is, the great body of the people, must necessarily fall, unless government takes some pains to prevent it.[3]

Any attempt to comprehend Smith's assessment of commercial society[4] would lead one to observe that, rightly or wrongly, he supposed commercial society might flourish only at the

---

3   *Wealth of Nations*, Bk. V, Ch. I, Pt. III, Art. 2d, pp. 781–2.

4   The effect upon life of commercial society as such, or more generally of the scientific and industrial revolutions, was not an unfamiliar subject of serious discussion in the eighteenth century. Smith himself lectured on "the effects of a commercial spirit, on the government, temper, and manners of a people, whether good or bad, and the proper remedies" (*Lectures*, pp. 172–3). Montesquieu discussed the same problem in the *Spirit of Laws*. And in 1750, when Rousseau was the laureate of the Academy of Dijon, the prize subject for the year was, Has the restoration of the arts and sciences had a purifying effect upon morals? Smith's unpromising conclusions, specified below, do not conflict with those of other philosophers of the age. Cf. Rousseau's *Discourse* on the Academy of Dijon's prize subject for 1750.

expense of the intellectual, social, and martial virtues of the mass of men. He was indeed on this account led to compare civilization with barbarism to the considerable disadvantage of the former,[5] arguing that "the understandings of the greater part of men are necessarily formed by their ordinary employments," with the result that in civilized societies, characterized by extensive division of labor, the mass of the people fall into a "drowsy stupidity" which the members of a rude society avoid owing largely to the variety of their regular activities. If we imagine that his qualification "unless government takes some pains to prevent [the ill effects]" thereof led to a genuine remedy, we have the means at hand to dispel the idea; for the species of "literary" education that he recommends for the poor goes no farther than reading, writing, and arithmetic, and "the elementary parts of geometry and mechanics"[6] which would have what we now call a vocational bearing. And as for remedying the "mental mutilation, deformity, and wretchedness, which cowardice necessarily involves in it,"[7] Smith can say no more of it than that it "would still deserve the most serious attention of government."[8] His conviction as to its practical insolubility as a problem of life is attested by his proposal that the defense of society be committed to the hands of a standing army of professional soldiers. And after all possible had been said about popular education, "the same thing" (viz., that it would still deserve the most serious attention of government) "may be said of the gross ignorance and stupidity which, in a civilized society, seem so frequently to benumb the understandings of all the inferior ranks of people."[9]

Turning from the laboring poor to the crucial class of merchants and manufacturers, which in the matured commercial society would include "all people of small or middling for-

---

5   *Wealth of Nations*, Bk. V, Ch. I, Pt. III, Art. II, p. 782–3.

6   Ibid., Bk. V, Ch. I, Pt. III, Art. II, p. 785.

7   Ibid., Bk. V, Ch. I, Pt. III, Art. II, p. 787.

8   Ibid., Bk. V, Ch. I, Pt. III, Art. II, p. 787.

9   Ibid., Bk. V, Ch. I, Pt. III, Art. II, p. 788.

tunes,"[10] we find them strangely handled by the great apologist of commerce. The famous conclusion to Book I of the *Wealth of Nations* is, so far as it concerns the merchants and manufacturers, an uncompromising castigation, ending with charges of deceit and oppression practiced upon the public.[11] Smith reflects upon "the sneaking arts of underling tradesmen" in almost the same passage that adverts to "the impertinent jealousy" and "the mean rapacity, the monopolizing spirit of merchants and manufacturers."[12] We are reminded of his reference to "[t]he merchants and artificers . . . (who) acted merely from a view to their own interest, and in pursuit of their own pedlar principle of turning a penny wherever a penny was to be got."[13] The whole acquisitive activity, to the reader's intense amazement, is reproved as "vulgar."[14] And the merchant (or at least the great merchant), is characterized as an indifferent citizen, "not necessarily the citizen of any particular country"[15] but rather in the category of

> [t]he proprietor of stock [who] is properly a citizen of the world,[16] and is not necessarily attached to any particular country. He would be apt to abandon the country in which he was exposed to a vexatious inquisition, in order to be assessed to a burdensome tax, and would remove his stock to some other country where he could either carry on his business, or enjoy his fortune more at his ease.[17]

---

10 Ibid., Bk. I, Ch. IX, p. 113.
11 Ibid., Bk. I, conc., pp. 266–7.
12 Ibid., Bk. IV, Ch. III, Pt. II, p. 493.
13 Ibid., Bk. III, Ch. IV, p. 422.
14 Ibid., Bk. II, Ch. III, p. 342.
15 Ibid., Bk. III, Ch. IV, p. 426.
16 I.e., is not a citizen.
17 *Wealth of Nations*, Bk. V, Ch. II, Pt. II, Art. 2d, p. 848–9. See also ibid., Bk. II, Ch. V, p. 365; Bk. V, Ch. II, Pt. II, Art. IV, p. 906; Bk. V, Ch. III, p. 927. Somewhat similar circumstances to those contemplated by Smith have produced troublesome "flights of capital" in our own time.

To this bill of particulars must be added the reasons given above disqualifying merchants and manufacturers for rule.[18] Together they display the nature and effects of those "irresistible moral causes" afflicting the mercantile order. A defect of patriotism, and, primarily, a defect of magnanimity seem to be the fatal shortcomings of this class from the point of view of morality. Yet the merchants and manufacturers are the carriers of the commercial principle, indispensable to civilization, whose presence, physical and moral, permeates commercial society.

For the completeness of the account, it should be repeated here that magnanimity is the peculiar attribute of barbarism as distinguished from civilization, in Smith's exposition.

Smith's criticism of the way of life of commercial civilization is extensive, embracing as it does the overwhelming mass of the population, and of course it is uttered in behalf of virtue. In spite of the elaborate theoretical array intended to install commerce as the realistic substitute for virtue in society, Smith demurs from the conclusion that the substitution succeeded. If he had denied that cowardice was vice, or that stupidity was undesirable, we might say simply that he had come to terms with the hard facts of theory and retained no serious reservations about the excellence of commercialism. But the truth is that he condemned cowardice, illiberality, and stupidity in the mass, and that he outright – perhaps unjustly – attributed these defects to commercial civilization as such. The theory that commerce is a substitute for virtue is thereby called into question, or more exactly, the ultimate indispensability of virtue is maintained even in the face of commerce itself.

We are confronted with a curious ambivalence in Smith's attitude toward the system of which he is the most renowned protagonist. If we take no more account of his criticism of commercialism than merely to state it and pass on, we leave his entire teaching essentially unintelligible. That he advocated commercialism and did so seriously, is not to be questioned. His purpose in having done so when he thought that he perceived gross moral shortcomings in commercialism is of

---

18   See above, pp. 78 ff.

the essence of his teaching.[19] Even if only to resolve a superficial inconsistency, it would be useful to penetrate this seeming paradox in Smith's teaching by searching for the true vindication of commercial society. But we might go further and say that the crucial ambivalence in Smith's attitude towards commercialism is precisely, what suggests that there is a "true" vindication of that system; that the system is vindicated by some end which it is meant to procure to mankind; and that Smith's own criticism of it in the name of virtue shows that the commercial system of society follows from a moral theory which is not Smith's last word on morality. For the commercial system is consistent with his moral theory. We are in the presence, therefore, of a system properly inferred from certain theoretical principles of morality, a system which is declared by its maker to be morally imperfect. If we can discover the true end of the system, we shall have discovered the *raison d'être* of the theory which forms the foundation of the system, and we shall also possess an intelligible explanation of Smith's ambivalence toward commerce.

We have implied that the commercial principle and system were advanced for the sake of some end, and we have at the same time implied that the moral theory which is the source of commercialism is necessarily also for the sake of that end. Our present task is to define the end, or in other words, to state Smith's intention in theorizing and inferring as he did.

Smith's criticism of commercial society is delivered in the name of virtue, and it arises from his conception of the reduced quality of life in purely commercial society. Yet when we reflect upon the morality to which he objects, we cannot fail to realize that it is his own moral philosophy which has in a sense forced it upon us, or rendered it inevitable, by reject-

---

19 It goes without saying that what is of importance to us in this connection is what Smith thought were the merits and defects of commercial society rather than the truth about it, should the two differ. Clearly, his position is comprehensible only in terms of what he perceived, and the norms of his science – the principles that govern the scientist's recommendations for disposing of humanity – become clear only when we concentrate on the considerations which he inwardly balanced against each other.

ing its antidotes. The real choice, after all is said, had been between society somehow based upon the principle of virtue and society based upon some substitute for virtue, such as commerce; or in terms of the discussion in Chapter I above, between polity incorporating the human moral order and polity incorporating the simply natural moral order. The reasons for Smith's rejection of the virtuous society are not obscure, but on the contrary, are openly displayed. When he rejected casuistry, or theological morality, he banished from society that dread of powers invisible which he repeatedly associated with "popular enthusiasm and superstition." When he rejected benevolence, he did so with his eye upon the magistrate, that power visible whom he would have deprived of all executive discretion if possible. Rejection of casuistry, the principle of duty supported by religion; and rejection of benevolence, or duty supported by the power of the prince, together left "justice" in unchallenged supremacy over society. But justice itself was made out of the same cloth with equality and freedom, as we have seen in the second chapter of this essay. Had not Adam Smith desired to emerge at this point, he need not have rejected duty or virtue as the principle of society. When he sowed these theoretical seeds, his harvest was not only the freedom and enlightenment which he desired, but the defect of moral, intellectual, and martial virtues which was a pest of tares in his garden. Justice as he defines it is compatible with, indeed requires, the freest republican government;[20] and this very justice, the substitute for and ouster of benevolence, is at the same time the soul of commerce.[21] In order to elevate strictly commutative justice to be the ruling principle of polity, and thus to guarantee freedom, it was necessary for Smith to obviate duty and virtue. His reprobation of the moral and intellectual defects of commercial society may be regarded as the tokens of his regret over the price that must be paid for humane, civilized life as he understood it. We cannot forget Smith's identification of civilization with the highest form of "social" or what is sometimes called socio-economic devel-

---

20 See above, p. 75.

21 *The Merchant of Venice* deals particularly with this subject.

opment. Civilization and commerce he thought were insepa-
rably joined. This precept is an enigma by itself, but is fully
intelligible when we realize that by civilization Smith meant
free, secular society, attainable only where commerce (i.e.,
competition) replaces the spiritual and temporal masters of
life.

Adam Smith's moral and political philosophy proper
seems to have been created for the service of a principle of
social organization, that principle being freedom from
absolute civil and spiritual power. We may see further how his
"philosophy of history" in a sense dictated his general philosophy to him. It was not reason that overcame the disorderly
despotism of feudal Europe; nor was it reason that overcame
the dominion of "superstition." It was, on the contrary, nothing but "the gradual improvements of arts, manufactures, and
commerce, the same causes which destroyed the power of the
great barons, [which] destroyed in the same manner, through
the greater part of Europe, the whole temporal power of the
clergy."[22]

> [C]ommerce and manufactures gradually introduced
> order and good government, and with them, the lib-
> erty and security of individuals, among the inhabi-
> tants of the country, who had before lived almost in a
> continual state of war with their neighbours, and of
> servile dependence upon their superiors. This, though
> it has been the least observed, is by far the most
> important of all their effects.[23]

Only by the workings of interest, given scope by commerce
and manufactures, could civilization supplant medieval barbarism. Commerce rather than conviction was the efficient
cause of the liberation of Europe. It is precisely because of the
efficacy of commerce in generating civilization that commerce
and civilization come to be identified. And it is precisely
because of this power of commerce to generate civilization

---

22 *Wealth of Nations*, Bk. V, Ch. I, Pt. III, Art. 3d, p. 803.
23 Ibid., Bk. III, Ch. IV, p. 412.

that Smith can conscientiously advocate commerce in spite of what he takes to be its radical defects.

Stated most generally, Smith's position may be interpreted to mean that commerce generates freedom and civilization, and at the same time free institutions are indispensable to the preservation of commerce. If the advantages of commerce can be sufficiently impressed upon the general mind, freedom and civilization will automatically follow in its train, and mankind will perhaps even be disposed to defend civilization, not necessarily out of love for freedom but out of love for commerce and gain.

That capitalism and free society have much in common has long been acknowledged, and has long been known to be in some way a part of Adam Smith's teaching. One general understanding of the relation between capitalism and free society (apart from Smith's doctrines) has been that classic advocates of freedom have, in important cases, espoused it for the sake of capitalism. I wish to suggest on the other hand that Smith may be understood as a writer who advocated capitalism for the sake of freedom, civil and ecclesiastical. More precisely, he may be understood as having advocated capitalism because in it he thought he recognized the instrument for reconciling civil and ecclesiastical freedom, as has already been shown, a difficult reconciliation which most of the tradition of Europe rejected as neither feasible nor desirable.

It is well known that Adam Smith regularly described commercial society as the "natural" order of society. The designation fits not only in the obvious sense that *laissez faire* allows nature to take its course with a minimum of human intervention. In fact, in the absence of a clear definition of nature at the outset, i.e., of the course that nature takes, the statement by itself is quite void of meaning. More significantly, the natural system defines morally imperfect society, and that for the reason that nature is itself morally imperfect. The distinction between the natural and the more perfectly moral, which leads to the tension between nature and superior morality, when nature is identified with preservation, was illustrated in the first chapter of this essay. The most emphatically natural system, upon that principle, will incorporate in the most pointed way the moral imperfection of nature itself. In effect, a close study of the *Theory of Moral Sentiments* would have suggested that its author would advocate a polity which, if it corresponded with his theoretical conception of the natural, would appear to him morally imperfect. Smith's application of the term "natural" to commercial society is best understood in this sense, in which it becomes entirely consistent with his critique of commerce in the *Wealth of Nations*.

In the light of these reflections, we may at last address the question, What is the real end of Smithian society, preservation or liberalism? We are bound to say that preservation is the true end of man by nature, but that the natural end is not *the* end. Nature seeks life, but man creates a criterion of the good life. The natural end as it is conceived by Smith is of course insufficient. It is liberalism, not preservation, that stands out finally as *the* end of social life – the artificial end not opposed to, but superimposed upon, the natural end as Smith comprehended it. Nature, in sum, becomes the means to a non-natural, supra-natural end constructed by man.

We were led to seek out Smith's intention by the presence of a sort of discordance among certain elements of his doctrine. The discord can be distinguished from gross self-contradiction only if we know Smith's purpose in writing. That unknown, the ambivalence of his attitude towards capitalism makes his advocacy of it unintelligible. In presenting his intention in this light, we have deliberately overstated it. If it be granted that free, secular society was his overmastering goal, there is no need to deny that he believed capitalism would also produce a rich and powerful society, and that he believed wealth and defensive might were necessary to civilization. We need not suppose that he was trifling with the reader when he eulogized the commercial principle as giving civilized peasants the material advantage over barbarian princes. Undoubtedly he sought through capitalism the enrichment of the people for the sake of their comfort and convenience; and undoubtedly he saw in capitalism the means of insuring the viability of the state – riches and power both being vital ends of polity. We need not here review the elements in Smith's doctrine that signify his participation with the modern philosophers in a realistic policy: concentration upon viability rather than excellence in individual and state alike.[24] It is sufficient for us to acknowledge that he looked for these things also, as ends to be wrought by capitalism, without affirming that they were the highest good which he sought to bring forth by his work. Nor is it without importance to us that Smith conceived the wealth of capitalistic society to be the source of its power to defend itself;[25] whereby he implied the divorcement through capitalism of virtue and viability, two entities thought inseparable even as late as the eighteenth century.[26]

There is a corollary to our thesis as to Smith's intention in advocating capitalism, one which we can do little more than mention here but which deserves at least that attention. Certainly since the appearance of Weber's *The Protestant Ethic and the Spirit of Capitalism*, the idea has prevailed that a relation exists between the relaxation of ecclesiastical authority and the practical triumph of capitalism. It is necessary to avoid vulgarizing a serious work, but at the same time it is necessary to be brief: nor need we do more than state a widely held view that purports to descend from Weber's thesis. It is that, in so far as the two phenomena are related, it is the relaxation of ecclesiastical authority that was procured for the sake of the commercial principle. Our statement of Smith's intention, however, indicates that for Smith, at least, the converse proposition represents the truth: the commercial principle was procured for the sake of effecting the relaxation of ecclesiastical authority. The subject is one that would clearly require extensive independent treatment, yet the following is tentatively offered: that in so far as Adam Smith reflects the main tradition of modern political philosophy (and the first chapter

---

24 See Leo Strauss, *Political Philosophy of Hobbes*, pp. 161–3, wherein is described the basis for the preoccupation of modern political philosophy with foreign policy.

25 A well-regulated standing army . . . as it can best be maintained by an opulent and civilized nation, so it can alone defend such a nation against the invasion of a poor and barbarous neighbour" (*Wealth of Nations*, Bk. V, Ch. I, Pt. I, p. 705–6).

26 Rousseau, *First Discourse*.

above seeks to suggest by how much he does so), modern thought generally sought commerce for the sake of relaxed ecclesiastical authority, and not the latter for the sake of the former.

The existence of such an "intention" on the part of Adam Smith informs us that capitalism was designed as a means to an end, rather than as an end in itself. Others must decide whether the end was worthy to be chosen, and whether the means are well adapted to the end; whether civil and ecclesiastical freedom together are worthy of choice as the end of society, and whether capitalism is the means wherewith to procure it. But beside these questions one truth stands out quite clearly: before one attempts to answer them, one can scarcely come to a sound conclusion as to the ultimate merits of the liberal commercial principle. As the means to an end, that principle must be judged not simply from the point of view of its intrinsic qualities, but in the light of the fact that it is intended to serve as the stay of general liberty, which is the end.

With or without an understanding of Smith's intention, the liberal principle has been defeated in a large part of the world and is under attack elsewhere, a situation which we frequently speak of as the crisis of liberalism. Our first impulse is to seek out the susceptibilities of liberalism which made even temporary defeat possible, and while moving in this direction we may long remain within the limits of Smith's own thought. Smith's critique of the commercial principle, made from the point of view of virtue, must now be recalled for the sake of the light it casts on our present subject. The criticism of one principle from the point of view of another of course implies the tension of the two – a tension which in the present case was established when Smith elucidated the opposition of nature and excellence.[27] Nature meant preservation, and it meant society, the means to preservation. Nature, society, and preservation were shown to be in conflict with excellence. Smith elected to orient life not upon excellence but upon preservation, albeit for the sake of liberty. His criticism of a

27   See above, pp. 43 ff.

society directly oriented upon preservation implicitly raises this question: Is preservation after all the natural end of life? Is it at last true that *nature* prescribes no norm of existence except existence itself; or is there such a thing as excellence, standing as a norm by which existence itself may be judged and qualified? If there is such a norm, then existence as such might be expected to give place to good or right existence as the aim of society.[28]

We might defend Adam Smith against his own implications by calling this to mind: that even if preservation is rendered questionable as the end of society, a reflection is created merely upon commerce, not upon the end to which the commercial principle is the means. Or in other words, supposing that commerce, the activity of indefinitely amassing the means of existence, is questioned as a natural principle of social life; and supposing further that it is questioned in the name of human excellence: does that at all affect the supreme end, Liberty, for the sake of which commerce is enthroned? We find ourselves still pursued by Smith's critique on behalf of excellence. There might be immense difficulties in the way of

---

28   It may be argued that it is idle even to think of a terrestrial end supervening over life because, lacking life, one would be incapable of seeking that or any other end. But such an argument mistakenly identifies the necessary condition and the end. It is true that a man must be alive in order to be aware of ends and to seek them; it by no means follows that the end may not be something other than life. If the end were living well or nobly, nothing would be easier to imagine than a conflict between the requirements of preservation and the requirements of man's end. The death in battle of every courageous soldier, and the self-sacrifice of all those who have died for high causes, testify to this fact of human life. It seems, therefore, that knowing how to live includes knowing how to die, and living well includes dying well; for although life does not include death, living does include dying: dying is an act of the living man, albeit his last one. Like all his other acts, it is intelligible as well or ill done, and especially where life *or* death is the practical alternative. But the simple possibility of dying well when life is an alternative contradicts the view that preservation comprises the good or the end for man.

understanding the content of excellence, but however the content of it may be understood, excellence is itself intelligible as inherently good, as the word naming it implies. Liberty is unintelligible except as liberty or freedom to do certain acts. Thus there is freedom to despoil one's neighbor, to overturn the state, and to inaugurate despotism, as well as to worship unhindered, to speak openly, and to speculate safely. In each case not "freedom," but despoiling one's neighbor, overturning the state, and so on, is the end. So that the mere implication of the existence of excellence, which is intelligible as an end, raises questions as to the intelligibility of Liberty as an end, within the framework of Adam Smith's teaching.

We pass in conclusion to a question which was raised not by Adam Smith but by his great contemporary and acquaintance, Rousseau. On the premise that the ideas of the mass of mankind descend to them from the superior ranks who are trained in universities, Smith proposed that the universities be employed as instruments for the broadcast dissemination of science and philosophy, the antidotes to superstition and enthusiasm and the props of free government. In his *Discourse* on the effect of modern developments in the arts and sciences,[29] Rousseau suggests that science itself is endangered by its broadcast dissemination. Fortunately, we are not called upon to affirm or deny this; but consider it we must, even if only hypothetically. For what if Rousseau were not entirely mistaken? What if "the herd of textbook authors, who have removed those impediments which nature purposely laid in the way to the Temple of the Muses"[30] should, by their activity, corrupt science itself by creating the illusion of understanding where none exists? What is there to prevent corrupted science from being perfectly disseminated, and how are we to assure ourselves that the dissemination of corrupted science may not be as dangerous to reason and freedom as ever ignorance itself could be? And with cruelest irony of all, what if vulgarized science should traduce Adam Smith himself, obscuring his purposes and making his design the miscon-

---

29 In the last few pages of the essay.

30 *Discourse on the Arts and Sciences*, Everyman ed., p. 152.

strued object of interested approbation or ignorant calumny? Precisely because the dispersive career of opinions is as he described it, the purity of what is dispersed as science must be defended by every means, or the crisis of our time will surely end in the cataclysm of science and liberalism together. Of all the problems of commercial society, this is perhaps the sharpest. It suggests the price that Smith had to pay when he purchased Freedom with an enlightenment linked with passion. The nature of the bargain is what is now being tested by the experience of our epoch.

CHAPTER IV
ADAM SMITH AND POLITICAL PHILOSOPHY*

The major writing of Adam Smith is contained in two books, *Theory of Moral Sentiments* (1759) and *An Inquiry into the Nature and Causes of the Wealth of Nations* (1776), to which may be added the posthumously published *Essays on Philosophical Subjects*. His major professional employment was to serve as professor of moral philosophy from 1752 to 1763 in the University of Glasgow, following the single session in which he held the chair of logic and *belles lettres*. His fame now rests upon the foundation he laid for the science of economics. In all of this there is not much of political philosophy to be seen, even allowing for the inclusion of jurisprudence in the Morals course. Smith's contribution to economics, however, has the character of a description and advocacy of the system now called liberal capitalism; and the ligaments between the economic order and the political system, close under any circumstances, are exceptionally broad and strong in the world as seen and molded by Adam Smith. The close conjunction of economics and political philosophy, even or perhaps especially if tending toward the eclipse of the latter, is a powerful fact of political philosophy; the men, like Smith, who were responsible for it would have a place in the chronicle of political philosophy on that ground alone.

---

*   Reprinted from *History of Political Philosophy*, eds. Leo Strauss and Joseph Cropsey, first edition, Chicago: Rand McNally, 1963.

Smith is of interest for his share in the deflection of political philosophy toward economics and for his famous elaboration of the principles of free enterprise or liberal capitalism. By virtue of the latter, he has earned the right to be known as an architect of our present system of society. For that title, however, he has a rival in Locke, whose writing antedated his own by roughly a century. Our thesis will be that, although Smith follows in the tradition of which Locke is a great figure, yet a distinct and important change fell upon that tradition, a change that Smith helped bring about; that to understand modern capitalism adequately, it is necessary to grasp the "Smithian" change in the Lockean tradition; and that to understand the ground of engagement between capitalism and post-capitalistic doctrines – primarily the Marxian – one must grasp the issues of capitalism in the altered form they received from Adam Smith. To state the point in barest simplicity: Smith's teaching contains that formulation of capitalist doctrine in which many of the fundamental issues are recognizably those on which post-capitalism contests the field.

It would be vastly misleading to suggest that the initiative in modifying the classic modern doctrine was Smith's. To avoid that intimation, we must cover all of what follows with a single remark on the obligation of Smith to his senior friend and compatriot, David Hume. Smith's moral philosophy, as he in effect admits, is a refinement upon Hume's which differs from it in respects that, although very significant, are not decisive.[1] A thorough study of the relation between the doctrines of Smith and Hume would disclose in full the connection between liberal capitalism and the "sceptical" or "scientific" principles upon which Hume wished to found all philosophy. The broadest conclusions that would emerge from such a study can be deduced from an examination of Smith's doc-

---

1   *Theory of Moral Sentiments* (1759), Pt. VII, Sect. II, Ch. III. Comparison of such a representative passage from Hume as part V of *An Enquiry Concerning the Principles of Morals* with, for example, part I of *Theory of Moral Sentiments* will suggest the broad agreement between the two doctrines.

trines alone; precisely those which do reflect so deeply the influence of Hume.

Many of Smith's fundamental reflections are contained in the *Theory of Moral Sentiments,* wherein he sets forth his important understanding of nature and human nature. He does this in the course of answering the following question: What is virtue, and what makes it eligible? The premise of his answer is that, whatever virtue may turn out to be, it must have very much in common with, perhaps it must simply coincide with, that by reason of which men or their actions deserve approbation. The question, What is virtue? is never distinct from the question, What deserves approbation? Approbation and disapprobation are bestowed upon actions. The spring of any action is the sentiment (or emotion, or affection, or passion – they are synonymous) which is the motive for committing the act. Approbation of any action must ascend to the passion which truly explains the action.

> The sentiment or affection of the heart from which any action proceeds, and upon which its whole virtue or vice must ultimately depend, may be considered under two different aspects, or in two different relations; first, in relation to the cause which excites it, or the motive which gives occasion to it; and secondly, in relation to the end which it proposes, or the effect which it tends to produce.
>
> In the suitableness or unsuitableness, in the proportion or disproportion which the affection seems to bear to the cause or object which excites it, consists the propriety or impropriety, the decency or ungracefulness of the consequent action.
>
> In the beneficial or hurtful nature of the effects which the affection aims at, or tends to produce, consists the merit or demerit of the action, the qualities by which it is entitled to reward, or is deserving of punishment.[2]

Propriety and merit are thus the attributes of the passion

---

2   Ibid., Pt. I, Sect. I, Ch. 3, p. 18.

behind each action that determine the virtuousness of the action. These bear a certain similarity to the "agreeable and useful" of Hume, but Smith believed his own doctrine to be original in that it avoids the final reduction of all approbation to utility, which Smith rejected on the Humean ground that "utility" is not as such recognizable by immediate sense and feeling, but only by a sort of calculation of reason. Smith believed he had been able to ground morality on a phenomenon of the passions alone, a belief to which the name of his book testifies. If sense and feeling are indeed immediate – unmediated in the sense that nothing is between them and the root of the fundamental self – then there is considerable value in bringing down the analysis of the virtues to its true bottom in the passions. In Smith's doctrine, the clue to that reduction is in the phenomenon of Sympathy, the criterion of propriety and merit.

Sympathy is a word used by Smith in its literal meaning, an etymological parallel of compassion: "feeling with," or a fellow feeling. It is a fact, of which perhaps no further mechanical account can be given, that the passions of one human being are transferred to another by the force of imagination at work in the recipient. The man who sees or merely conceives the terror, hatred, benevolence, or gratitude of another must to some extent enter into that passion and experience it himself, for he must imagine himself in the other's circumstances, and therefrom everything follows. Of chief importance in the foregoing is the qualification "to some extent." If the impartial spectator, cognizant of what stimulated the terror, hatred, or other passion of the agent, feels in his own breast the same measure of that passion as moved the agent to his action, then the spectator literally sympathizes with the agent and approves his act as consistent with "propriety." The spectator experiences sympathetically the passion of the agent; and if he experiences it in the same degree, he further experiences the "sentiment of approbation" – for that, too, is a passion.

Propriety, however, is not the only ground of moral virtue. Not only the suitableness of the agent's passion to its cause, but the aim or tendency of that passion, its effect, has a bearing on the moral quality of the act in question. Smith refers to "the nature of the effects which the affection aims at, or tends to produce." The "or" is disjunctive, and we must later discuss the important difference between the effects that the sentiment aims at and those that the act it inspires actually tends to produce. For the present it is enough to note that when an action falls upon some human being, it will cause him to feel gratitude or resentment because it will be either beneficial or harmful, pleasurable or painful. If an impartial spectator, informed of all the circumstances, would sympathize with the gratitude felt by the object human being, then the spectator would judge the agent's act to be meritorious, and the second condition of moral virtue would have been met. In brief: if the actual or supposed impartial spectator should sympathize with the passion both of the agent (propriety) and of the patient (merit), then the agent's act may be pronounced virtuous on the basis of the spectator's feeling of approbation.

If Smith's elaboration of the sympathy mechanism did nothing more than show how a rather strict morality could be educed from the passions and the imagination alone, it would have a certain interest. In fact, it points toward a much wider circle of consequences. Sympathy cannot be separated, in Smith's formulation, from imagination. Together they define an undoubted natural sociality of man. By the exercise of two sub-rational capacities, sympathy and imagination, each man is by his nature led or compelled to transcend his very self and, without indeed being able to feel the other man's feeling, is able and is driven to imagine himself in the place of that other and to participate, how vicariously is a matter of indifference, in the feelings which are the fundamental phenomena of the other's existence. Smith, it will be recalled, wished to know not only what virtue is but what makes it eligible. Why – in principle – do men choose to be virtuous, when to be virtuous means to be deserving of approbation? Smith's answer is that it is of the nature of a human being to desire the approbation and love of his human congeners.[3] The first sentence of

---

3 'The chief part of human happiness arises from the consciousness of being beloved." *Theory of Moral Sentiments*, Pt. I, Ch. V, p. 41.

the *Theory of Moral Sentiments* intimates the withdrawal that is in progress from the doctrine of the war of all against all: "How selfish soever man may be supposed, there are evidently some principles in his nature, which interest him in the fortune of others, and render their happiness necessary to him, though he derives nothing from it except the pleasure of seeing it." The combination of imagination, sympathy, and the need for the love and approbation of other men is the ground for Smith's asseverations that nature formed man for society.[4]

Not only does Smith thus teach a natural sociality of man, but also the natural character of the moral law. He can with ease refer to "the natural principles of right and wrong"[5] understanding by "right" not merely what benefits or avoids bringing harm to the agent. He can do so because the ground of moral action and perception is the inner constitution of human nature; not in the antique sense of man's highest possibilities, it is true, but in the sense of human psychology – the instincts, sentiments, mechanisms of sympathy that are the efficient causes of human behavior. These are perfectly natural, and the sentiments of approbation are equally so; hence the principles of right and wrong are incontestably natural.

Smith's version of natural right depends very heavily upon the construct of the "impartial spectator," the imaginary being who is supposed to represent all mankind in viewing and judging each individual's actions. Judgment rendered from such a point of view implies that no man may rightly prefer himself to the extent of making exceptions from the general rule in his own behalf. "As to love our neighbour as we love ourselves is the great law of Christianity, so it is the great precept of nature to love ourselves only as we love our neighbor, or what comes to the same thing, as our neighbour is found capable of loving us."[6] Recourse to the imagined judgment of general humanity at the same time directs conscience toward the imagined surveillance maintained over each man at all times by a supposed all-seeing humanity. The

---

4   Ibid., Pt. III, Ch. I, pp. 109–13.
5   Ibid., Pt. V, Ch. II, p. 200.
6   *Theory of Moral Sentiments*, Pt. I, Ch. V, p. 25.

constructive standard of "universal mankind" is fundamental to the version of natural right and natural sociality taught by Smith. It is also a premonition of the post-capitalistic construct of "all mankind" as the focus of right and history.

It is true that Smith taught the natural sociality of man and the natural basis of the moral law, but this modification of the modern natural law doctrine did not mean a return to antiquity. It must be repeated that natural right for Smith rests upon the primacy of the sub-rational part of the soul, and that natural sociality as he understood it is not an irreducible principle of man but the product of a mechanism at work. Later on, Kant was to speak of the same phenomenon as man's asocial sociality. Natural sociality in this sense does not, as it did for Aristotle, point toward political society. It rather resembles gregariousness. It is a compassion with one's fellow species-members that has everything in common with the alleged unwillingness of horses to tread upon a living body (of any species) and the distress of all animals in passing by the cadavers of their like.[7] To claim on the basis of it that man is by nature a social animal is by no means to claim equally that he is a political animal. Man is tied to humanity by the bonds of immediate sense and feeling, but he is tied to his fellow citizens as such by the weaker, superinduced, bonds of calculation or reason, derivative from considerations of utility. As we have seen, the viewpoint of moral judgment for Smith is that of "man" or universal mankind, the homogeneous class of species-fellows. The moral law is natural in such a sense as to overleap the intermediate, artificial frontiers of political society and regard primarily the natural individual and the natural species. Under that law, the perfection of human nature is "to feel much for others and little for ourselves, . . . to restrain our selfish, and to indulge our benevolent affections. . . ."[8]

---

7 From Rousseau, *Discourse of the Origin of Inequality*, First Part. Readers of Rousseau's two Discourses will be struck by the similarity of themes and views between them and the *Theory of Moral Sentiments*. The division of human nature between self-love and compassion, and the qualified goodness of civil society are but instances.

8 *Theory of Moral Sentiments*, Pt. I, Sect. I, Ch. V, p. 25.

Political society, however, is not directed toward this humane perfection of human nature but toward the safeguard of justice very narrowly conceived. "Mere justice, is upon most occasions, but a negative virtue, and only hinders us from hurting our neighbour. The man who barely abstains from violating either the person, or the estate, or the reputation of his neighbours, has surely very little positive merit." Justice means to do "every thing which [a person's] equals can with propriety force him to do, or which they can punish him for not doing."[9] Justice, in brief, closely resembles compliance with the law of nature as seen by Hobbes and Locke. Smith understood it so himself. He concluded the *Theory of Moral Sentiments* with a passage on natural jurisprudence, justice, and the rules of natural equity, meaning by all of them "a system of those principles which ought to run through, and be the foundation of the laws of all nations." (He closes by promising to take up this theme in a later work. His only other book is *The Wealth of Nations*.)[10]

We shall not sufficiently understand Smith's version of man's natural sociality if we do not grasp thoroughly the difference between man conceived as a social animal and as a political animal. It is helpful for this purpose to consider further the problem of justice, the singularly political virtue which might even be synonymous with obeying the positive law. Justice, in the context of Smith's moral theory, is a defective virtue. He prepares for the exceptional treatment of justice by dividing moral philosophy into two parts, ethics and jurisprudence, the subject of the latter being justice. The defence of justice means the punishment of injustice; and the

---

9   Ibid., Pt. II, Sect. I, Ch. I, p. 82.

10   In Letter 248 addressed to Rochefoucauld, dated I Nov. 1785 Smith indicated that he still had two works "upon the anvil": "the one is a sort of philosophical history of all the different branches of literature, of philosophy, poetry and eloquence: the other is a sort of history of law and government." The advertisement to the 6th edition of the *Moral Sentiments* repeats the promise made at the close of the first, despite Smith's advanced age.

punishment of injustice is based upon the unsocial passion of resentment, the desire to return evil for evil, the command of "the sacred and necessary law of retaliation" which "seems to be the great law which is dictated to us by Nature."[11] Political society is based upon a moral paradox, one of many we will encounter: sociality rests upon latent animosity, without which the state could not exist.

In the second place, justice, equal to rendering another no less (or more) than what is his due, does not command gratitude and therefore in Smith's system is not attended with merit – or with "very little." Considering both the nature of justice and the safeguard of it, it is a defective virtue in that it cannot, or almost cannot, deserve fullest approbation, on the grounds of merit as well as propriety.

In the third place, although there is a sense in which political society is natural, it is a weak sense. The national society is indeed the protector and the matrix of ourselves, our homes, our kin, our friends, and Smith does not for an instant dream of the withering away of the state. "It is by nature endeared to us." But "the love of our own nation often disposes us to view, with most malignant jealousy and envy, the prosperity and aggrandisement of any other neighbouring nation."[12]

> The love of our own country seems not to be derived from the love of mankind. The former sentiment is altogether independent of the latter, and seems sometimes even to dispose us to act inconsistently with it. France may contain, perhaps, near three times the number of inhabitants which Great Britain contains. In the great society of mankind, therefore, the prosperity of France should appear to be an object of much greater importance than that of Great Britain. The British subject, however, who, upon that account, should prefer upon all occasions the prosperity of the

---

11 *Theory of Moral Sentiments*, Pt. II, Sect. I, Ch. II, p. 71; cf. Pt. II, Sect. II, Ch. II, p. 84.

12 Ibid., Pt. VI, Sect. II, Ch. II, p. 228.

former to that of the latter country, would not be
thought a good citizen of Great Britain. We do not love
our country as a part of the great society of mankind:
we love it for its own sake, and independently of any
such consideration.[13]

These reservations and qualifications upon political sociality
deserve notice. They will appear in a swollen incarnation con-
jured by Marx a century later, when the replacement of political man by the species-animal reaches a climax.

It would be misleading to suggest that Smith's doctrine of
man's sociality was a relapse into the Middle Ages or into
antiquity. It would be more misleading to suggest that, in
Smith's view, human nature is simply dominated by a natural
sociality of any description. We have given attention to the
mechanical or psychological bond of sympathy, at the basis of
Smith's moral theory, in order to show the change in emphasis between the preparation of capitalism in Locke's doctrine
and the elaboration of it in Smith's. But the theme of man's
natural directedness toward preservation is not by any means
made to languish by Smith. On the contrary: "self-preservation, and the propagation of the species, are the great ends
which Nature seems to have proposed in the formation of all
animals."[14] There is no reason to doubt that Smith meant this
in all its force. We are able to gather, therefore, that if we use
"altruism" and "egoism" in their literal sense, man can be
described, according to Smith, as being by nature altruistic
and egoistic – a species-member moved by love of self and fellow feeling with others.

It is one of the outstanding characteristics of Smith's system that sociality, withal of a certain description, and self-cen-
tered concentration upon preservation, are shown as profoundly combined in a natural articulation of great strength;
and this is achieved simultaneously with a rehabilitation of
morality upon natural grounds: "Nature, indeed, seems to
have so happily adjusted our sentiments of approbation and

---

13   Ibid., Pt. VI, Sect. II, Ch. II, p. 229.
14   Ibid., Pt. II, Sect. I, Ch. V, p. 77n.

disapprobation, to the conveniency both of the individual and of the society, that after the strictest examination it will be found, I believe, that this is universally the case."[15] When it is borne in mind that Smith's teaching aims at the articulation of morality and preservation, and that the practical fruits of his doctrine are intended to be gathered by emancipating men, under mild government, to seek their happiness freely according to their individual desires, the accomplishment as a whole commands great respect. The reconciliation of the private good and the common good by the medium not of coercion but of freedom, on a basis of moral duty, had perhaps never been seen before.

In this wide and symmetrical edifice Smith perceived what appeared to him to be an irregularity or a class of irregularities. He observed that at certain points a disjunction develops between what man would by nature be led to approve as virtuous and what he is led by nature to approve as conducive to the preservation of society and the human species; and this notwithstanding the over-all truth of the passage quoted immediately above. It will be recalled that the elements of a virtuous act are propriety and merit, and that both rest upon a ground of sympathy. If men did not desire the sympathy of others, as well as respond to the impulse to sympathize with them, there would be no morality and no society. But the natural tendency of men is to sympathize especially with joy and good fortune; and it goes without saying that men not only desire to be sympathized with but to be sympathized with by reason of their prosperity, not their adversity. But the wish to be sympathized with on the grandest scale becomes, as a consequence, the foundation of ambition, which is the aspiration to be conspicuous, grand, and admired. To this aspiration the multitude of mankind lends itself, for it naturally sympathizes with eminence, that is, wealth and rank. But wealth and rank are not, as Smith occasionally said, necessarily conjoined with wisdom and virtue. He remarks, "This disposition to admire, and almost to worship, the rich and the powerful, and to despise or, at least, to neglect persons of poor and mean condition, though necessary both to estab-

---

15   Ibid., Pt. IV, Sect. I, Ch. II, p. 188.

lish and to maintain the distinction of ranks and the order of society, is, at the same time, the great and most universal cause of the corruption of our moral sentiments."[16]

Merit, we remember, is the quality of an act that the impartial spectator would pronounce worthy of gratitude. The decisive quality of such an act is the propriety of the agent's passion in committing it, his benevolent intent toward the patient, and the patient's pleasure in the benefit conferred, in consequence of which he desires to reciprocate a benefit to the agent. The conjunction is perhaps complicated, but through it all one condition stands out clearly: benefit must be conferred on the patient. Now Smith observes that there is a gap of sorts between the intention and the consummation. That gap is Chance. Because of mere chance good will miscarries, and the benevolent agent produces nothing or worse than nothing for his intended beneficiary. On other occasions the agent, intending nothing or possibly worse than nothing, happens to be the source of a benefit to the patient. Contrary to sound morality, the first agent's act goes without the approval of sympathy and the stamp of virtue, while the second agent's act wins applause and gratitude. The universal tendency of men to regard the issue rather than the intention is said by Smith to be a "salutary and useful irregularity in human sentiments," for two reasons. In the first place, "to punish ... for the affections of the heart only, where no crime has been committed, is the most insolent and barbarous tyranny." To try to live a common life while holding men culpable or laudable for their secret intentions would mean that "every court of judicature would become a real inquisition." In the second place, "Man was made for action, and to promote by the exertion of his faculties such changes in the external circumstances both of himself and others, as may seem most favorable to the happiness of all. He must not be satisfied with indolent benevolence, nor fancy himself the friend of mankind, because in his heart he wishes well to the prosperity of the world."[17] Smith goes on to speak of the utility to the world of the cognate inclination men

---

16   Ibid., Pt. I, Sect. III, Ch. III, p. 61.
17   Ibid., Pt. II, Sect. III, Ch. III, p. 106.

have, to be troubled in spirit even when the ill they have wrought is wholly unintended, a subject that he illuminates with some healthy remarks upon the fallacious sense of guilt, illustrated by the "distress" of Oedipus. In sum, nature has wisely provided that our sentiments direct us toward the preservation of our kind where a conflict between preservation and either moral virtue or sound reason is brought on by the divergence of intent and issue.

Further in the same vein, Smith notes that when a man conquers fear and pain by the noble exertion of self-command, he is entitled to be compensated with a sense of his own virtue, in exchange for the relief and safety he might have had by giving way to his passions. But it is the wise provision of nature that he be only imperfectly compensated, lest he have no reason to listen to the call of fear and pain and to respond to their promptings. Fear and pain are instruments of preservation; a man or a species indifferent to them would die. The self-command that dominates them does not, as it ought not, bring with it a sense of self-esteem sufficient to outweigh the anguish of suppressing those violent passions.[18] Evidently moral virtue neither is nor ought to be simply its own reward; nor therefore can it be unqualifiedly eligible or eligible for its own sake. It must yield, according to the dictate of nature, a certain precedence to preservation.

In an important passage, Smith unfolds further the paradox of natural morality as he conceives it. He is led to contrast "the natural course of things" with "the natural sentiments of mankind."[19] It is in the natural course of things that industrious knaves should prosper while indolent men of honor starve, that great combinations of men should overweigh small ones, and finally that "violence and artifice prevail over sincerity and justice." The natural sentiments of man, however, are in rebellion against the natural course of things: sorrow, grief, rage, compassion for the oppressed, and at last despair of seeing the condign retribution of vice and injustice in this world – these are man's natural sentiments. The natural course

---

18   Ibid., Pt. III, Ch. I, pp. 110–11.
19   Ibid., Pt. III, Ch. V, pp. 168–69.

of events, though, for all its offensiveness, has something weighty to recommend it. In allotting to each virtue, without favor or accommodation, the reward proper to it, nature has adopted the rule "useful and proper for rousing the industry and attention of mankind." Toil and moil happen to be indispensable to human survival, and the only way to draw them forth is by appropriate reward and punishment. The natural course of events supports the preservation of the race at the expense of precise morality; the natural sentiments of mankind are stirred by "the love of virtue, and by the abhorrence of vice and injustice." Nature is divided, but not equally divided against itself. The cause of unmitigated virtue can be heard only upon a change of venue to a jurisdiction in a world beyond nature.

Smith pursues his theme of the price in goodness and reason that must be paid to get the world's fundamental business done. He takes up the question, of much importance to his doctrine, whether the utility of actions is the basis of their being approved. If the answer were a simple affirmative, then it would follow that the principle of virtue (approbation) is rational: the calculation of usefulness. But we know that in his view the principle of virtue and approbation is not reason but sentiment and feeling, via sympathy. Yet it is evident that mankind exhibits a steady tendency toward those measures of labour and government which are the supports for the preservation of the race. Smith explains this by recurring to a delusion imposed upon men by nature, a delusion that does the work of reason better than reason could have done it. When we look upon the power or wealth in a man's possession, our minds are led in imagination to conceive the fitness of those objects to perform their respective functions. At the same time we sympathize with the imagined satisfaction of the possessors of those prizes. It is only a step from that to desiring ourselves to be happy in greatness, and thence to putting forth the immense exertions that eventuate in wealth and government. Upon consideration, it appears that we are led to pursue prosperity and power by a psychological motive, and thus to generate wealth and order among men as by-products of subjective "drives," as we would say. Moreover, and conjunctively, we act under the influence of the appetite for the means to gratification, not even for the gratification itself, when we seek after wealth and power. Both are desirable for the happiness they supposedly give their possessors. In fact, happiness is not at all, or very little, promoted by the possession of power and riches, those "enormous and operose machines contrived to produce a few trifling conveniencies to the body, consisting of springs the most nice and delicate, which must be kept in order with the most anxious attention, and which in spite of all our care are ready every moment to burst into pieces, and to crush in their ruins their unfortunate possessor."[20]

Smith's reason for depreciating distinction of wealth and place is of interest: "In what constitutes the real happiness of human life, [the poor and obscure] are in no respect inferior to those who would seem so much above them. In ease of the body and peace of the mind, all the different ranks of life are nearly upon a level, and the beggar, who suns himself by the side of the highway, possesses that security which kings are fighting for."[21] It is in this context that Smith announces, in the *Theory of Moral Sentiments,* the notion of the expression of the "invisible hand," very famous from its elaboration through the central argument of *The Wealth of Nations.* The passage deserves extensive quotation:

> And it is well that nature imposes upon us in this manner. It is this deception which rouses and keeps in continual motion the industry of mankind. It is this which first prompted them to cultivate the ground, to build houses, to found cities and commonwealths, and to invent and improve all the sciences and arts, which ennoble and embellish human life: which have entirely changed the whole face of the globe, have turned the rude forests of nature into agreeable and fertile plains, and made the trackless and barren ocean a new fund of subsistence, and the great high road of communication to the different nations of the earth.

20 *Theory of Moral Sentiments,* Pt. IV, Ch. I, pp. 182–83.
21 Ibid., Pt. IV, Ch. I, p. 185.

The earth by these labours of mankind has been obliged to redouble her natural fertility, and to maintain a greater multitude of inhabitants. It is to no purpose, that the proud and unfeeling landlord views his extensive fields, and without a thought for the wants of his brethren, in imagination consumes himself the whole harvest that grows upon them. The homely and vulgar proverb, that the eye is larger than the belly, was never more fully verified than with regard to him. The capacity of his stomach bears no proportion to the immensity of his desires, and will receive no more than that of the meanest peasant. The rest he is obliged to distribute among those, who prepare, in the nicest manner, that little which he himself makes use of, among those who fit up the palace in which this little is to be consumed, among those who provide and keep in order all the different baubles and trinkets which are employed in the oeconomy of greatness; all of whom thus derive from his luxury and caprice, that share of the necessaries of life, which they would in vain have expected from his humanity or his justice. The produce of the soil maintains at all times nearly that number of inhabitants which it is capable of maintaining. The rich only select from the heap what is most precious and agreeable. They consume little more than the poor, and in spite of their natural selfishness and rapacity, though they mean only their own conveniency, though the sole end which they propose from the labours of all the thousands whom they employ, be the gratification of their own vain and insatiable desires, they divide with the poor the produce of all their improvements. They are led by an invisible hand to make nearly the same distribution of the necessaries of life which would have been made, had the earth been divided into equal portions among all its inhabitants, and thus without intending it, without knowing it, advance the interest of society, and afford means to the multiplication of the species.[22]

---

22   Ibid., Pt. IV, Ch. I, p. 185.

Beyond this there is no advantage in multiplying the evidence of Smith's belief that the dominant end of nature with respect to man, namely, the prosperity of the species as a whole, is achieved by mitigations of morality and reason. Since this is a point which post-capitalistic thought was to take up polemically and against which it was to bring its ultimate, most ambitious dialectic, it deserves to be examined with some attention.

That nature's end for man is advanced by the guidance of his sentiments rather than his reason follows from the premise that the passions are more governing than the mind, and every animal persistently desires its own uninterrupted being. A man's nature is more immediately reflected in what he feels than what he thinks; moreover, the difference between the two is not the profound one anciently conceived but is rather such as can be composed by their being both subsumed under "perceptions." Smith does not employ the language of "impressions and ideas" used by Hume in the enterprise by which the operation of the mind was given a unified appearance as the distinctions among sensation, emotion, and reason were blurred. If Smith had done so, he would more explicitly have concurred in Hume's definition of the self as "that succession of related ideas and impressions, of which we have an intimate memory" and of "ideas [as] the faint images of [impressions] in thinking and reason."[23] The reduction of the self, the ego or the real man, to his actuality or to the traces of what he has actually perceived rather than to his soul and its powers or "faculties" is part of the doctrine that rejected innate ideas and therewith all but the nominal essences. This doctrine, with its echoes of Hobbes and Locke, is interlaced with the view that the lines of force along which nature produces and communicates its motions penetrate him and govern him more through his passions than through his reason.[24]

---

23   Hume, *A Treatise of Human Nature*, I.I.i. and II.I.ii.

24   Hume's remark is characteristically uncompromising: "[the reason] can never oppose passion in the direction of the will" (*Ibid.*, II.III). Smith makes two remarks, in the form of allusions, which deny man's unique rationality: "mankind, as well as ... all other rational creatures" (*Theory of Moral Sentiments*, Pt. III, Ch. V, p.

In any event, Smith's formulation is that nature did not leave it to man's feeble reason to discover that and how he ought to preserve himself, but gave him sharp appetites for the means to his survival as well as for survival itself, thus ensuring his preservation. But it is this same primacy of sentiment over reason, or at least the equal subsumption of them both under something like perception, that is the basis for the concessions which must be made against morality on behalf of preservation.

It will be recalled that Smith's moral doctrine begins with approbation: the virtuous is so because it is in fact or in principle approved by the sentiment of mankind. We now understand that a difficulty exists because nature teaches man to approve both what conduces to morality and what conduces to preservation. The instruction of nature is occasionally equivocal. Evidently the attempt to derive the Ought from the Is is vexed by the fact that, although what is virtuous is actually approved, it does not follow either that everything which is approved is virtuous or that everything which is virtuous is approved. It is from this circumstance that the "irregularities" or concessions previously mentioned have their origin. What, then, is to be gained by the psychological or "behavioral" derivation of a natural morality? It is that by this method, moral virtue may be deduced from the character of "man as man," i.e., in abstraction from his character as a political being and attentive only to his character as a "natural" one. Smith's moral philosophy aims at comprehending the basis of virtue as that basis may be said to exist in a fully actual state at every moment in "the bulk of mankind"[25] as such. That is to say, Smith's starting point is the natural equality of men in the sense elaborated by Hobbes. The contrast with classical antiquity throws light on the modern position. The famous scheme of Plato's *Republic* makes a high principle of the division of labor or distribution of functions in the political society because virtue in one social class could not well be measured

166.) and the great society of all "rational and sensible beings" (*Ibid.*, Pt. VI, Sect. II, Ch. III, p. 237.)

25   *Theory of Moral Sentiments*, Pt. III, Ch. V, p. 162.

by the same rule against which it must be measured in another class. Aristotle's *Politics* distinguishes the virtue of slaves, freemen, and men of excellence; the *Nicomachean Ethics* cannot be regarded as a manual of the excellence of the bulk of mankind. The ancient moralists coldly concentrated upon the distinction between the politically weighty people and the entire populace that dwelt within the frontiers. Only democracy has the merit of making possible the effacement of that distinction, and we are entitled to deem the "humanization" of moral virtue – its universalization or reference to what is actually present in "all men as men" – as the democratization of morality.

Democracy is the regime that minimizes the distinction between rulers and ruled, the fundamental political phenomenon; and in that sense it can be said that democracy or liberal democracy tends to replace political life by sociality (private lives lived in contiguity) at the same time as it diffuses political authority most widely. The abstraction of morality from the demands of political life proper is in a way impossible: political life has to be lived, and support for it must be provided in the form of economic organization, the use of force for suppressing crime and rebellion, the legitimation of conventional inequalities in the interest of order, and so on. Where morality is radically "human" or "natural" in the sense of those words that is opposed to political, the indispensable provision for political life will have the character of an inroad on morality, or an irregularity. It is not our contention that the moral basis of Smith's social doctrine is contrived to produce an abstraction from the conditions of political existence. It is rather, on the contrary, that in order to mitigate or forestall that abstraction, which his premises threaten to enforce, he must have recourse to "irregularities" of nature or exceptions to his premises.

There is hardly a better way of illustrating the elusive relation between rectitude and politics than by the following passage from Churchill's *Marlborough:*

> The second debate in the Lords . . . drew from Marlborough his most memorable Parliamentary performance. It is the more remarkable because, although

he had made up his mind what ought to be done and what he meant to do, his handling of the debate was at once spontaneous, dissimulating, and entirely successful. As on the battlefield, he changed his course very quickly indeed and spread a web of manoeuvre before his opponents. He made candour serve the purpose of falsehood, and in the guise of reluctantly blurting out the whole truth threw his assailants into complete and baffling error. Under the impulse of an emotion which could not have been wholly assumed, he made a revelation of war policy which effectively misled not only the Opposition but the whole House, and which also played its part in misleading the foreign enemy, who were of course soon apprised of the public debate. He acted thus in the interests of right strategy and of the common cause as he conceived them. He was accustomed by the conditions under which he fought to be continually deceiving friends for their good and foes for their bane; but the speed and ease with which this particular manoeuvre was conceived and accomplished in the unfamiliar atmosphere of Parliamentary debate opens to us some of the secret depths of his artful yet benevolent mind.[26]

It is apparent that dissimulation cannot be made the principle of morals; it is also apparent that morality which makes no serviceable distinction between dissimulation in a noble cause and common mendacity will end either in the precisianism that condemns it all as vice or in the latitudinarianism that peers unsuccessfully for the line between vice and virtue. Ancient moral philosophy could in this respect be described as very politic. It recognized in prudence a subtle virtue that animated the others from its seat in the mind. In palliation of the Odysseanism of the ancients' moralizing, it should be said that departure from the straitest morality was countenanced by them in the ultimate interest of something higher, for they did

---

26 Winston S. Churchill, *Marlborough: His Life and Times* (4 vols. in 2 books, 1 947), Vol. III, Bk. II, p. 303. Reproduced by permission of Charles Scribner's Sons and George Harrap & Co., Ltd.

not conceive moral excellence to be the greatest of all excellences. The Smithian subtractions from morality cannot be in the interest of anything higher, for there is nothing higher: "The most sublime speculation of the contemplative philosopher can scarce compensate the neglect of the smallest active duty."[27] "The man who acts solely from a regard to what is right and fit to be done, from a regard to what is the proper object of esteem and approbation, though these sentiments should never be bestowed upon him, acts from the most sublime and godlike motive which human nature is even capable of conceiving."[28] To state the case somewhat simplistically, the ancients and the moderns alike conceded something in mitigation of strict moral virtue, the ancients without repining because they had in view a higher excellence, Smith with mixed feelings because his aim could not exceed moral virtue in worth.

Smith's aim, a free, reasonable, comfortable, and tolerant life for the whole species, found its hope, its basis, and its expression in the science of economics as he to a considerable extent launched it. Anything like a detailed account of Smith's economics would be far out of place here, and we shall confine ourselves to selected themes. His teaching in *The Wealth of Nations* is above all famous for its defence of free enterprise on a broad and simple line: The welfare of the nation cannot be separated from its wealth, which he conceives in the modern mode as the annual national product. But the annual product of the nation is the sum of the annual products of the individual inhabitants. Each inhabitant has an undying interest in maximizing his own product and will do everything possible to accomplish this if left in freedom. Thus all should be accorded this freedom, and they will simultaneously maximize the aggregate product and keep each other in check by the power of competition. His renowned attack on mercantilistic capitalism – the system of invidious preference for the merchant interest – is part of his argument that the common interest is served not by differential legislative stimulation of enterprises

---

27 *Theory of Moral Sentiments*, Pt. VI, Sect. II, Ch. III, p. 237.
28 Ibid., Pt. VII, Sect. II, Ch. IV, p. 311.

but by allowing nature automatically to convert the individual self-interest into the good of all:

> As every individual, therefore, endeavours as much as he can both to employ his capital in the support of domestic industry, and so to direct that industry that its produce may be of the greatest value; every individual necessarily labours to render the annual revenue of the society as great as he can. He generally, indeed, neither intends to promote the public interest, nor knows how much he is promoting it. By preferring the support of domestic to that of foreign industry, he intends only his own security; and by directing that industry in such a manner as its produce may be of the greatest value, he intends only his own gain, and he is in this, as in many other cases, led by an invisible hand to promote an end which was no part of his intention. Nor is it always the worse for the society that it was no part of it. By pursuing his own interest he frequently promotes that of the society more effectually than when he really intends to promote it. I have never known much good done by those who affected to trade for the public good. It is an affectation, indeed, not very common among merchants, and very few words need be employed in dissuading them from it.[29]

We have no difficulty recognizing the natural reconciliation of the individual and common interest for which the *Theory of Moral Sentiments* has prepared us. Nor are we unprepared for the moral "irregularities" that Smith conceived to be incidental to that reconciliation. They fall under two or three main heads in the argument of *The Wealth of Nations*. In the first place, the prosperity of each and all cannot be disconnected from their productivity, and their productivity rests upon the division of labor. But the division of labor inevitably

---

29 *An Inquiry into the Nature and Causes of the Wealth of Nations* (Indianapolis, IN: Liberty Fund, 1981), Bk. IV, Ch. II, p. 456. All references are to this edition.

stultifies the working classes, much if not the bulk of mankind. The laborer's "dexterity at his own particular trade seems . . . to be acquired at the expense of his intellectual, social, and martial virtues. But in every improved and civilized society this is the state into which the labouring poor, that is, the great body of the people, must necessarily fall, unless government takes some pains to prevent it."[30] In his discussions he tries not to exaggerate the likelihood that the government will succeed.

In the second place, a large part if not the preponderant part of the economic life of the nation must come under the regulation of the class of merchants and manufacturers. His animadversions upon them as a body of men are sometimes shockingly severe. The burden of his objection against them is that their preoccupation with gain puts them in illiberal conflict with the other orders of society and with the nation as a whole – except by inadvertence.[31] The wisdom of government is necessary to prevent their mischief, i.e., their interested interference, and to give free rein only to their useful activities, i.e., their productiveness. Smith was not the dogmatist that some advocates of *laissez-faire* were later to become.

In the third place, the annual addition to product is believed by Smith to be generated by labor. The "exchangeable value" or price of each commodity, once land has been made private property and capital has been accumulated, "resolves itself" into wages, rent, and profit. In this way, landowners and the employers of labor "share" in the produce of labor. Smith is at pains to argue that the profits of capital are not a wage for the "supposed labour of inspection and direction," which he said is often "committed to some principal clerk."[32] He was far from attempting to conceal the contribution to output that results from the accumulation of capital. On the contrary, he dwelt upon it; but he described it as taking effect by

30 *Wealth of Nations*, Bk. V, Ch. I, Art. II, p. 782.

31 Ibid., Bk. I, Ch. IX, pp. 108–9; Bk. IV, Ch. III, p. 493.

32 Ibid., Bk. I, Ch. VI, p. 66.

an improvement in the "productive powers of labour."[33] In the course of his investigations into what we now call national income accounting, he certainly gave later generations some reason to regard him as holding a labor theory of value, with concomitant beliefs about distribution. As for rent, that is "a monopoly price"[34] for the use of land, by the exaction of which the owner is enabled to share in the annual product of labor. We cannot fail to notice how little trouble Smith gave himself to justify this "sharing" and this "resolving." On the contrary, by a certain invidiousness of expression – "As soon as the land of any country has all become private property, the landlords, like all other men, love to reap where they never sowed, and demand a rent even for its natural produce"[35] – he indicates a reserve as to its perfect propriety. He seems to think, it is true, that when the facts of distribution are recited, the intimation of possible inequities may be fully balanced by a statement of the broad, compensatory benefits: he speculates whether it might not be true "that the accommodation of a European prince does not always so much exceed that of an industrious and frugal peasant, as the accommodation of the latter exceeds that of many an African king, the absolute master of the lives and liberties of ten thousand naked savages."[36] But Smith manifestly did not imagine himself to be addressing the multitude of laboring poor in detailed defence of capitalism, as Marx was to address them in detailed denunciation. Smith freely hinted at his notion that something like one of his moral "irregularities" lay around the root of the distributive order, but it was much outweighed by the correlative advantages for all – and he loathed the men of "system" who would be incapable of grasping such a simple computation.

Smith did not refer to the complex of free enterprise as "capitalism" but as "the system of natural liberty," or the condition in which "things were left to follow their natural course,

33   Ibid., Bk. II, Ch. II, p. 287.
34   Ibid., Bk. I, Ch. XI, p. 161.
35   Ibid., Bk. I, Ch. VI, p. 67.
36   Ibid., Bk. 1, Ch. 1, p. 24.

where there was perfect liberty."[37] Nature meant for Smith the humanly unhindered or unobstructed, and this more amply means what is not confounded by the misplaced interventions of human reason: letting nature take its course, letting men do as they are instinctively prompted to do, as far as that is compatible with "the security of the whole society."[38] It is easy to conceive and to grant that natural is in distinction to artificial, human, or constrained to obey a forecontrived design. Thus freedom is all on the side of nature, as opposed to constraint on the side of human reason. At the same time, however, nothing in the world is so unyielding and hence constraining as the necessary dictate of deaf and dumb nature, while the source of man's freedom resides in his power of reason, the origin of his various contrivances.[39] Smith's manner of confronting this difficulty is in effect to declare for the freedom of reason harnessed in the service of the more binding freedom of nature: calculation at the command of passion. Smith's doctrine is pervaded by the consequences of the fact that the superordinate element, nature conceived as the free motive of passion, is the symbol of man's unfreedom, as Kant was to emphasize so elaborately.

It is a distinguishing characteristic of Smith's doctrine and of liberal capitalism at large that they do not conceive freedom to be important primarily because it is the condition for every man's existence as an individual moral being, the ground of his self-legislating will in action or of his humanity. Liberty continued to mean for Smith what it had meant to Locke, to Aristotle, and to the long tradition of political philosophy: the condition of men under lawful governors who respect the persons and property of the governed, the latter having to consent to the arrangement in one way or another. This view of

---

37   Ibid., Bk. IV, Ch. IX, p. 687; Bk. I, Ch. X, p. 116.

38   Ibid., Bk. II, Ch. II, p. 324.

39   Smith commonly juxtaposes "naturally" and "necessarily," the latter often used apparently as an intensified form of the former. Cf., e.g., ibid.; Bk. I, Ch. VIII, p. 104; Bk. III, Ch. I, p. 377; Bk. IV, Ch. I, p. 445–46; Bk. IV, Ch. II, pp. 454–55; Bk. IV, Ch. VII, Pt. III, pp. 626–67; Bk. V, Ch. I, Pt. III, p. 802.

liberty is primarily political and belongs to the libertarianism of Locke, not of Rousseau. The capitalistic project is not animated by a search for methods of institutionally liberating the inner drives of every man in the interest of the moral will. It is animated by a search for methods of institutionally liberating every man's natural instinct of self-preservation in the interest of external, politically intelligible freedom and peaceful prosperous life for mankind as a whole. Therefore Smith had no difficulty in conceiving man as free while both in thrall to nature and subject to forms of law which guarantee his external freedom but can scarcely aim to be the basis of his internal emancipation from that same nature.

Smith is thus at liberty to repose his trust in a wisdom of nature that shows itself even or especially in the folly and injustice of man: the moral hygiene that produces a multitude, in fact a race of self-legislators, was not indispensable to his plan, nor was political life a species of psychotherapy for bringing on man's subpolitical emancipation. Smith was thus resigned to receive the benefits of civil society even if they must be mediated by certain undoubted ills, and he was prepared to do so indefinitely if the benefits are vast and the ills unavoidable. In this respect he anticipated the mechanisms of philosophy of history as it would emerge, but not its ends: good through ill and reason through folly, but no Elysium at a rainbow's end.

It is important for us to see more exactly what Smith's doctrine has in common with philosophy of history as that was later to develop. There is, to begin with, his belief in a "natural progress of things toward improvement" – animated by "the uniform, constant and uninterrupted effort of every man to better his condition," bettering his condition being understood in "the most vulgar" sense.[40] Smith illustrates this in an account of the progress of Europe from medieval disorder to the comparative regularity of modern times. The anarchy of old persisted because the great landed proprietors had troops of retainers who comprised, in fact, private armies. Nothing could produce order which did not dissolve those armies. The

---

40   *Wealth of Nations*, Bk. II, Ch. III, p. 343.

basis for their existence was the fact that the grandees had abundant income in kind which, under the primitive conditions of commerce then prevailing, they could not dispose of by exchange or sale. They accordingly were compelled to feed it to crowds of men who became their dependents and inevitably their soldiers. What brought down the entire system was the enlargement of trade, which enabled the magnates to convert their produce into money and thence into luxuries for their personal delectation instead of into the military basis of their political power.

> A revolution of the greatest importance to the public happiness, was in this manner brought about by two different orders of people, who had not the least intention to serve the public. To gratify the most childish vanity was the sole motive of the great proprietors. The merchants and artificers, much less ridiculous, acted merely from a view to their own interest, and in pursuit of their own pedlar principle of turning a penny wherever a penny was to be got. Neither of them had either knowledge or foresight of that great revolution which the folly of the one, and the industry of the other, was gradually bringing about.[41]

Smith speaks of the ascendancy of the Roman Church from the tenth to the thirteenth century. He regards it as signalized by the temporal power of the clergy, and that in turn as resting upon the influence of the clergy with the multitudes of men. The inferior ranks of people were bound to the clergy by ties of interest, the multitudes depending upon a charity which was bestowed freely because, once again, the clergy had no other means of disposing of an enormous produce from their lands. When such means presented themselves, the constitution of the Catholic Church underwent a profound alteration:

> Had this constitution been attacked by no other enemies but the feeble efforts of human reason, it must have endured for ever. But the immense and well-built fabric, which all the wisdom and virtue of man

---

41 Ibid., Bk. II. iv. p. 423.

> could never have shaken, much less overturned, was
> by the natural course of things, first weakened, and
> afterwards in part destroyed. . . .
>
> The gradual improvements of arts, manufactures, and
> commerce, the same causes which destroyed the
> power of the great barons, destroyed in the same man-
> ner, through the greater part of Europe, the whole
> power of the clergy.[42]

By these same instrumentalities, the species of mankind at
large is drawn together, probably upward as well as onward.
Smith regards the geographical discoveries as of unparalleled
significance for the species: "The discovery of America, and
that of a passage to the East Indies by the Cape of Good Hope,
are the two greatest and most important events recorded in the
history of mankind." The communication and commerce of
the species as a whole was thereby in principle achieved for
the first time in the memory of man, and with that epochal
event came the supreme occasion for enabling all mankind
reciprocally "to relieve one another's wants, to increase one
another's enjoyments, and to encourage one another's industry."[43]

Smith believed that, to a large extent, nature speaks to history in the language of economics, and that the broad course
of history so instructed is probably toward an easier, more cultivated, more rational, and secure life for the generality of
mankind. At the same time, he imagined that the advance of
civilization was synchronous with the generation of a tremendous industrial mob, deprived of nearly every admirable
human quality. Civilization is not an unqualified good, or
more accurately, it comes at a price. This famous theme, of
which Rousseau was the virtuoso, was developed by Smith
with concern but without agitation. He proposed to palliate
the ill with a wide system of almost gratis elementary school-
ing for the masses and with the encouragement of an unheard-
of number of religious sects (as many as three thousand), each

---

42   Ibid., Bk. V, Ch. I, Pt. III, Art. III, p. 803.
43   Ibid., Bk. IV, Ch. VII, p. 626; cf. Bk. IV, Ch. I, p. 448.

necessarily to be so small that every member of it would be conspicuous to the surveillance of his fellow communicants. All would maintain a vigil upon each other's morals that, far from being in any danger of flagging through lack of interest, would itself require to be moderated by febrifuges: courses of education in science and philosophy and artistic spectacles such as theatre.[44] Smith repeatedly recommends the intellectual and moral state of much of industrial mankind to the most serious attention of government, not only out of philanthropy but for obvious reasons of state.

Our thesis, with a summary of which we shall now conclude, has been this: Within a short time of the completion of Locke's work, intelligent men began to reflect on and to draw out what would today be called the "moral implications" of his doctrine.[45] How far he had mitigated Hobbes's teaching of the natural ferocity of man and thereby turned political philosophy in the direction of economics has been described elsewhere.[46] But the chief teaching of the modern school of natural law was not thereby impaired: nature continued univocally to mean preservation, with the supporting rights to whatever pertains thereto. Now this came to be regarded as insufficient, and the reduction of man to his affections was thought to imply that man is affected not only toward himself but toward his species. Perhaps Locke was not given enough credit for the important mitigation mentioned above, which is in this direction, but in any event the theme was made emphatic by Smith (at about the time of Rousseau's *Second Discourse*). The reduc-

---

44   Ibid., Bk. V, Ch. 1, Pt. III, Art. II, pp. 784–86; Bk. V, Ch. I, Pt. III, Art. III, pp. 795–97.

45   The reader's attention should be drawn to the work of Bernard Mandeville (c. 1670–1733) whose *The Fable of the Bees* (1714) had the subtitle "Private Vices, Public Benefits." Controversy raged around him, and Smith added his rebuke by dealing with him in a chapter "Of Licentious Systems" (*Theory of Moral Sentiments*, Pt. IV, Sect. II, Ch. IV), at the same time admitting that Mandeville was not mistaken in all respects.

46   For example in "John Locke" by Robert A. Goldwin, in *History of Political Philosophy*, ed. Leo Strauss and J. Cropsey (1963).

tion of human life to its emotional foundations was enlarged to become the ground of duties as well as rights. It cannot be denied that those duties were consciously made to revolve about the preservation of the species; but it cannot either be denied that duties are different from rights, and the two require somehow to be reconciled with one another. In the course of reconciling the duties of moral virtue with the rights of nature, which is to say preservation, Smith had recourse to the tension between nature and the moral order derived from it, leaving the reconciliation inevitably imperfect. From this germ grew the teaching as to the moral imperfection of the natural or best order of society – the free, prosperous, and tolerant civil society. In its self-understanding, capitalism thus anticipated the chief post-capitalistic criticism of capitalism: civil society is a defective solution of the human problem.

Our second point, inseparable from the first, is that the self-understanding of capitalism also anticipated an astonishing proportion of what was to be proposed by the nineteenth century as the alternative to capitalism. We have tried to show how the direction of capitalism was toward the construction of a universal mankind, both as the ground of duty (the universal spectator) and as the ultimate beneficiary of economic progress – thus as the ultimate society. The engine of that progress was the ignoble desires and strivings of man, channelled through the economic institutions of production and distribution that opened up to him from time to time. An expectation of good through evil, reason through unreason, progress, a belief in the tendency of the interest of mankind to supersede that of particular political society, in the preponderance of economic influence on human affairs, in the primacy of labour in the process of production, in the preoccupation of civil society with the defence of property, this and more which Marxism would trumpet was present to the doctrines of capitalism in one measure and form or another, as it has been our purpose to show. A strange light is cast on Marx's theory that capitalism contains the seed of its own negation. It might perhaps be said that according to its own self-understanding, the ground of capitalism coincides to a remarkable degree with the seed-bed of its own negation; but the seed itself is an alien thing, namely, philosophy of history, something that was generated not by the working of any economic institutions but by an act of human speculation.

Perhaps Smith is to be blamed for not having extracted a metaphysic from that "wisdom of nature" which he believed to guide the human process and to which he so often recurs, a metaphysic that would historicize the consummation of the whole human career. Perhaps he ought to have perceived the potency in such a metaphor as the "wisdom" of nature and gone on to postulate still higher wisdoms by which the laws of nature itself might be brought under orders. He never reached that point, however, for he did not question the belief that there is an unchanging horizon within which all change takes place, that horizon or framework being Nature.

Philosophy of history is outside our scope. For the present we may observe that when Rousseau's teaching of the malleability of human nature received its due cultivation and enlargement, it proved to be the little leaven that leavened the whole lump. The paradoxes and irregularities that liberal capitalism was willing to abide because of their origin in man's nature could not be tolerated by the nineteenth century since it no longer saw a need to tolerate them. The nature that gives rise to inconveniences must away, and itself submit to be superseded by the law of the change of nature, namely, History. It is this fissure, narrow but bottomless, that divides capitalism from communism.

CHAPTER V
THE INVISIBLE HAND: MORAL AND POLITICAL CONSIDERATIONS*

The bicentenary of *The Wealth of Nations* tends to be overshadowed by that of the United States. But the celebration of the country's past evokes, inevitably, reflections on its future, and to reflect on our future is to think of our institutions – of their stability and their prospects, thus the threats to them, and in turn the basis for those threats in the complaints so often voiced against commercial liberalism. The weightiest among those complaints, or the ones perhaps most often taken seriously, are moral: what are the rights and wrongs of commercial liberalism, what conception of justice does it elevate to authority, into what ways of life does it lead its participants? Evidently, speculation about our future draws heavily on thought about what we are, and thus about whence we are sprung. But our "whence" is, in some immeasurable degree, a past age's thoughts which have become our own conceptions and have become incarnated in our national ways and institutions. We are led from our political past through our actual present to our political prospect, and thence once more to the past, but this time to a past that lives in the pages of books. We find ourselves turning to *The Wealth of Nations* with a sense

---

*   Presented as a Harry Girvetz Memorial Lecture on the bicentennial of *The Wealth of Nations*, 19 February 1976, at the University of California at Santa Barbara.

that reflection on the literary bicentenary is important not only in its own right but as the necessary preparation for investigating the issues evoked by the more splendid political anniversary.

It would be at the very least inconvenient to discuss *The Wealth of Nations* without reaching an early understanding about the name by which to call the social system that the book is famous for advocating. Inattention could encourage falling in with the common practice of referring to it as capitalism; but what that name presupposes differs materially from Smith's conception of the system's essence, and the term should therefore not be used freely in this context. The name "capitalism" was employed by Marx in order to affirm that the essence of this social and economic system is the generation of profit ("surplus value.") Everything important for the manner of life in this society follows from the employment of labor through the purchase of labor-power by possessors of "capital." To call the system of free commerce "capitalism" is thus to imply that the essential characteristic of the social order is the existence of the conditions that generate or enhance profit as such. These conditions are conceived to include preeminently the division of the people into what are loosely called classes, especially the classes of those who do and those who do not own the means of production. But classes in this sense have no legal status; they have only a speculative or dialectical definition. In this respect, they do not differ from the "classes" of people who live on opposite sides of a street, or of the even numbers between zero and eleven. Referring to such groupings as classes rather than sets obscures the fact that they are arbitrary or convenient – designated for the purpose of pursuing a certain line of argument or speculation. On the other hand, a legal definition goes beyond a speculative one in that it carries a positive imputation of right. Thus there was an imputation of right – however misguided is not now relevant – in the legal definition of the class of slaves, while there is no imputation of right in the ratiocinative definition of dwellers on one side of a street, or of a set of numbers. Evidently, a large problem is opened up by attributing to "classes" a decisive political importance in a society that ignores them legally, and that officially imputes no right to their existence or to membership in them.

However worthy of being pursued to a conclusion, this theme was introduced not for itself but in order to strengthen the argument for finding a name for Smith's system that is harmonious with his conception of that system. Fortunately, he in fact gave it a name, one with as heavy a freight of meaning as is borne by "capitalism": the "system of natural liberty."[1] As the name suggests, and as *The Wealth of Nations* maintains, the essence of Smith's system is consistency with the dictate or tendency of nature, not either the generation of an invidious distributive share or the friction of interests present in a society composed of functioning parts. Marx insists on presenting free commerce as though its essence were conflict; Smith presents it as though its essence is a kind of sociality or collaboration. Our immediate task is not to judge between Smith and Marx but to improve our understanding of Smith's doctrine, which we can begin to do by thinking about his phrase, "natural liberty."

Natural liberty is either a tautology or a paradox. Suppose for a moment that in his primary state (primary either in time or in principle), man is unrestrained by anything external to himself that hinders his moving or acting. Then the restraints that now do hinder him must have imposed, as laws, conventions, practices, all have been imposed, by men on themselves. If the primary state is correctly called natural, then "natural" and "liberty" agree so well that the phrase resembles a tautology. Nature, or the primary, is the basis of freedom; artifice and convention are the grounds of constraint, and if freedom is accepted as the aim of society, then the effectual goal of society is to restore itself to nature, or to recapture nature through social institutions, or something to the same effect.

Simple or obvious as these notions might appear, they are full of difficulties. To begin with, the modification of society in the direction of nature – meaning by that the progressive weakening of the conventions and artifices that constrain – is

---

1   *Wealth of Nations*, Bk. IV, Ch. IX, p. 687.

tantamount to the weakening or even the dissolution of civil life. But the dissolution of civil life may well be equivalent to the dissolution of society itself, in which case the "naturalization" of society would be a misnomer for the dissolution of society. Then what began as a tautology would reveal itself as a contradiction: the attainment of society's essential goal, its naturalization and liberalization, would entail the dissolution of society. There is a way to avoid this outcome. Suppose that the modification of society in the direction of nature need not mean the weakening or discarding of conventions and artifices but rather the installation of "natural" conventions and artifices – human constructions that follow the indications of nature while still restraining men's movements. This suggestion will be intelligible if nature and artifice are mutually reconcilable – if man's making can be sufficiently guided by what man does not make. But why should not the products of two makers serve a single end, the end dictated by the one maker that comprehends the other? More concretely, suppose that the whole import of the artificial social construction is the recovery of natural liberty in the form of self-legislation. After all, the liberty of natural man consisted in a freedom to do whatever he desired to do, which appears to be the condition of a being that legislates for itself. Then the conventions of self-legislation would be those natural artifacts whose possibility we were questioning. Perhaps we could be satisfied with this if we were not conscious of a discord between doing what one desires to do and legislating for oneself. Doing what one desires means doing *whatever* one desires – now this and perhaps at another time something else; while self-legislation means to lay down laws that one obeys, and presumably always and steadily obeys, with the understanding that "obeys" carries with it not only constancy but the implication of an impulse that is to be overcome by obedience. But it is precisely the conquered impulse that comprises the "desire" in the expression, "to do as one desires." Self-legislation contradicts doing what one desires, and exists exactly in order to replace the rule of desire with the rule of something else, presumably something worthier, perhaps even something freer. It now appears that in progressing to the artifices that concur rather than conflict with nature, one reaches the point at which natural liberty again becomes confused: the institutions that follow those indications of nature which point to self-legislation clash with those indications of nature which consist in desire and in the impulse to act according to desire. Yet both sorts of institution or artifice can claim to give effect to freedom, indeed to natural freedom.

Perhaps we have reached confusion because we were not sufficiently precise in speaking of nature's indications, and of the sense in which man the artificer might be the agent of, or a fragment of nature, of the more comprehensive maker. More exactly, we have not faced the issue whether it is on the one hand responsiveness to desire or on the other hand self-legislation that nature sets forth as true "natural liberty." It is clear that nature cannot well teach both if self-legislation is the expression of man's freedom in a voluntary act to confine his desires.

If self-legislation is natural freedom, then obedience to the desires or instincts is natural bondage. Moreover, if self-legislation is natural freedom, then man's primary condition or natural state is bondage and not freedom, for subjection to (self-legislated) law presupposes a prior condition that calls for law. But in any case, why speak of obedience to desires or instincts as bondage? Because the desires and instincts move us as if, or perhaps literally, mechanically. Acting under mechanical impulsion or necessity is acting without intention or volition, thus acting without being the prime cause of one's acts. It is acting for causes that cannot be traced to one's own will. But as long as it remains unclear that a being that exists in the order of nature, as man does, *can* separate itself from the chain of natural causes sufficiently to act under the causation of its "will" alone, so long will the suspicion linger that the will is simply a construction or hypothesis, something hypostasised in order to underlie "freedom", as the soul might be called something hypostasised in order to underlie the motion and thought of otherwise inert body. On the assumption that every act (indeed every event) must have a cause, but that "freedom" requires that there be acts which are not caused in the usual sense, one posits a Will that is capable of causing acts in such a way that the odium of necessity does not cling to the acts and thereby deprive them, as mere responses to externality, of their possible morality. One could imagine that a settled determination to purge action of the moral contamination of simple causation might lead a thinker to conceive a weakening of the authority of the ordinary process of causation rather than to superimpose on that process an extraordinary, higher cause unlike any that operates wholly within the order of nature. In other words, one might expect a Hume to arise who would argue that causation is mysterious rather than absolute and unshakable, instead of expecting a Kant to arise who would introduce freedom of the will and the immortality of the soul as correctives outside the causal chain of natural necessity. Reflections on Hume and Kant at this point are not a luxury but rather are indicated because of the degree to which Hume's thought impinged on Smith's and some of Smith's understandings recommended themselves to Kant. In order to avoid leaving the impression that the questions of natural liberty, desire, and the action of the will need be discussed only in terms of the simple alternatives already presented, we should notice that Nietzsche, not an advocate for liberal commerce, rehabilitates instinct by *uniting it with the will,* and ascends to a freedom so intimately affiliated with creativity as to be within the reach of humanity on a plane beyond the grasp of society or of politics.

In this conspectus of possibilities, we must recognize one more before we turn thematically to Adam Smith, his system of natural liberty, and the invisible hand. It might be crucial to distinguish among the desires and passions when ascribing to nature certain unwilled causes of human action. According to a famous notion of Smith's contemporary, Rousseau, most of what we now possess as passion has been generated within society and does not belong to our pristine nature. Consequently, to gain ascendancy over hatred, envy, greed, or pride is not simply to master nature, or to acquire control over a process of natural causation in an unqualified sense, but is rather to find a means within the order of natural causes whereby to bring the powers of nature to bear upon or against one another for a moral, human end. But precisely if the present ensemble of human motivations that we think of as our natural apparatus had a genesis or history, the system of rewards, penalties, and incentives that we devise to govern our impulses is partly "natural" and partly only historical: "human nature" – what now is – is emphatically not coeval either with nature or with man. So far as Rousseau contemplates the adjustment of human nature as it now is to some more authoritative – more primitive, more free – natural norm, he does look for a norm "outside nature," outside what we now know to be, and what is for every practical purpose, our nature. But the prospect for finding a standpoint unequivocally and consciously outside nature in order to enable mankind to master nature in the interest of freedom and morality began with Kant, who elaborated for the purpose a metaphysics and a moral philosophy that stand or fall with the possibility that a realm of freedom, outside the realm of natural necessity, exists and is the scene of the action of the human will.

These remarks are prompted by the occurrence of the term "natural liberty" in the name that Smith applied to his system. They are intended to suggest that Smith's system should be regarded in its relation to a great structure of modern reflection on man's moral condition. That reflection had been brought on by the apprehension that a perfectly mechanized nature, of which humanity forms an integral part, will be graspable by man's mind exactly in proportion to the rule of regularity, predictability, or necessity in that nature. But the more necessary and knowable the natural world, the less free are the human ingredients of it, and the more painful the predicament of modern men, who see their science and their freedom as so grounded that each is a mortal threat to the other.

It is understandable that modern men should be especially afflicted with these apprehensions, for the modern age is emphatically the time of the flowering of natural science, which is a human consciousness of nature as a mechanism; and that consciousness has proved capable of becoming the consciousness not only of the whole chain of natural causes, but of man's place in that chain. Does consciousness of his place in the overwhelming chain of necessity enslave man; or does his higher self-consciousness, his consciousness of *his* consciousness of nature, emancipate him by elevating him above his condition? It is very hard to be sure whether a perfectly clear view of one's entanglement seals one's bondage or rather dissolves it; but it is easier to see that a slave who does not know himself to be one is not simply enslaved. The human being for whom natural science does not exist as the intimation of an infinite chain of causes is not aware of himself as integrated in such a chain. He is not aware that nature poses or constitutes a threat to his freedom; he is necessarily even less aware that his consciousness of his plight is (i.e., would be) *eo ipso* emancipation from his enslavement. He is unaware of these things because he is not a philosopher but a citizen – a fact that remains decisive until it is shown that the deepest thoughts available to an age seep into the average consciousness as *Zeitgeist.* In such a case, average men would have a feeling, perhaps a vague sense of unhappiness or detachment, but certainly not the clear and distinct understanding of their situation which is prerequisite to their enslavement, nor the clear consciousness of their own consciousness that is the condition for their emancipation from the bonds of nature. Failing a theoretical perception of the nature of things, what remains to a man is life within his horizons as these appear to him through his everyday existence. So far as the issue is freedom and bondage, those horizons are the horizons of the citizen, who as such thinks of his freedom and bondage in direct and immediate terms, which are political: is he or is he not in thrall to men who wield the state's power. But even if, or rather especially if there seeped into the average consciousness an unhappiness that reflects a philosophical conception of man as enthralled to nature, it would be folly or wickedness to represent that unhappiness as the product of political formations. Further, it would be absurd to hold out hope of emancipation at all unless there were means, which would have to be other than those of contemplation, for giving the mass of mankind an existence on a plane "outside of nature." But those means do not exist, and every nostrum offered under such a guise proves to be one kind or another of state organization or political regime. Thus the folly and wickedness are compounded, for the means of emancipation that are offered, being political, are represented to be effective against a bondage that has no political foundation at all but arises from man's inclusion in the infinite chain of natural causes.

The claims and offers that appear so problematical have indeed been made, and with great practical effect. They are directed, of course, against the system of thought and life engendered by Adam Smith. For the moment, we do not know how vulnerable Smith is to the attack. We have seen that he uses the term "natural liberty" with an innocence that is either thoughtless or farseeing, maintaining as it does a total silence about any possible tension between natural necessity and human freedom. In revolving that issue, I have tried to show that there is a sense in which there is no problem, and also a sense in which there would be no solution if there were a problem. There would be no problem, and if a problem no solution, if the problem and the solution would have to be political or practical rather than philosophic or contemplative. But Smith, in proceeding so directly to the compatibility of nature and liberty, appears to adopt what I have called the average man's posture or the horizon of the citizen. In doing so, has he avoided a spurious issue that has bemused much of modern thought, or has he overlooked a crucial condition that has vitiated much of modern life? If the former, his stature has never been properly acknowledged. If the latter, we can understand only too well the basis for those complaints against our institutions that disturb the celebration of our political bicentennial. Against the background of the issues so delineated, we turn to Smith's formula of the invisible hand.

Smith makes reference to the invisible hand in two places, in *Theory of Moral Sentiments* (1759), and in *Wealth of Nations* (1776). Let us look at the two passages.

> The produce of the soil maintains at all times nearly that number of inhabitants which it is capable of maintaining. The rich only select from the heap what is most precious and agreeable. They consume little more than the poor, and in spite of their natural selfishness and rapacity, though they mean only their own conveniency, though the sole end which they propose from the labors of all the thousands whom

they employ, be the gratification of their own vain and insatiable desires, they divide with the poor the produce of all their improvements. They are led by an invisible hand to make nearly the same distribution of the necessaries of life, which would have been made, had the earth been divided into equal portions among all its inhabitants, and thus without intending it, without knowing it, advance the interest of the society, and afford means to the multiplication of the species.[2]

As every individual, therefore, [naturally] endeavors as much as he can . . . to employ his capital in the support of domestic industry, and [necessarily] so to direct that industry that its produce may be of the greatest value; every individual necessarily labours to render the annual revenue of the society as great as he can. He generally, indeed, neither intends to promote the public interest, nor knows how much he is promoting it. By preferring the support of domestic to that of foreign industry, he intends only his own security; and by directing that industry in such a manner as its produce may be of the greatest value, he intends only his own gain, and he is in this, as in many other cases, led by an invisible hand to promote an end which was no part of his intention.[3]

It is clear that the invisible hand is not a metaphor for a power by which nature compels men to perform any acts. The invisible hand is a metaphor that certainly presupposes that men are compelled to respond in act to their natural selfishness and rapacity. It presupposes that men may be described as being in bondage to the compulsions of nature. But in contradistinction to what it presupposes, what it says is that something called nature transforms the ugliness and bondage of man into a true human good. Whatever else can be said, it seems obvious that Smith begins by conceding that man is a passive object, governed by and immersed in an overwhelm-

---

2 *Theory of Moral Sentiments*, Pt. IV, Ch. I, p. 184-5.
3 *Wealth of Nations*, Bk. IV, Ch. II, p. 456.

ing environing force, that he is part of a great chain of causes; and then Smith must find a way to extricate humanity from a desperate slavery that, in destroying freedom, threatens morality (what morality has an automaton?). The way that Smith finds for achieving these ends is the discovery of nature in its expanded amplitude. Nature is to begin with the inescapable causes of human actions. It then proves to be also the power that prescribes the remote ends of those actions and in addition causes those ends to materialize in fact, according to an intention that must be said to belong to it, nature, and not to the human actors. There is scarcely any way for us to avoid a deep sense of uneasiness brought on by the suspicion that Smith's nature is only too literally just that – Smith's construction: a rationalized wish.

Smith's vision of nature might be defective, but it does not differ from others in being a construction. No one has ever seen nature; what we see is the world, and from it we go on to arrive at nature, which is an explanation of the world. There can be no such thing as an account of the world as *nature* that does not go beyond the mere description of the phenomena as phenomena. But what is the philosopher free to add? Only what makes the world intelligible. And what can that mean? May Ideas be added to the phenomena? May God be added to the world, as if nature, the explanation, is itself a thing to be explained? Does this perplexity not reveal that the world to be explained might have to be seen as the sum of the phenomena and the explanations of the phenomena, with the consequence that not only the intelligibility of the world but the goodness of the comprehensive explanation for man, i.e., the goodness of the natural philosophy for man, becomes the criterion that governs the question, what is the philosopher free to add to the phenomena in order to arrive at nature? Whatever might be the answer to this question in general, with regard to Adam Smith it may be said confidently that he added compulsion and benevolent purpose to the world in order to arrive at nature. Man in nature is the subject of a benevolent despotism; nature is the despotism that, added to the world, makes it intelligible and, incidentally, good. I have come close to suggesting that natural philosophy can resemble high mythologizing. And I have come close to suggesting that Smith locates within the world, in order to constitute nature, what Biblical theology locates outside the world in order to explain what came to be called nature. Smith makes it unnecessary to look beyond nature – to a divine will above it, as Scripture teaches, or to a human will alongside it, as Kant teaches. What Smith achieves is the transposition of an ancient understanding that nature is exhaustive into the theoretical arena in which nature is thought to be wholly mechanical. When I say that Smith achieved this transposition, I do not mean to imply that he was the first to envision exhaustive mechanical nature. On the contrary, the clarity with which Spinoza, for example, perceived both the vision and the threat contained in it to freedom and morality, typifies the reason for modernity's insecurity in the embrace of nature. What I do mean to imply is that Smith's achievement gives us the decisive clue to the discovery of the decisive question for his system: what does it tell us about the status of man in nature supposed both exhaustive and mechanical?

The figure of the invisible hand brings to light the fact that, along with human bondage in nature goes the reconciliation of the selfish impulses with the good of many or all. If the individual and society and the species are fully integrated in comprehensive nature, then nature could be said to be taking care of her own in exploiting greed for the common advantage. But in so doing, nature appears to release every human being from a conscious concern with the happiness or good opinion of the rest of mankind. Certainly it is the intention of much of Smith's work to show the contrary. The invisible hand goes no further than to argue that, in matters of preservation – the production and distribution of the means of life – the repellent egoism of men is mechanically converted into actions useful to society and species. But Smith believed that he understood how, in important affairs of life that are not reducible to mere preservation, nature leavens the self-regard of men and converts it into virtue. In making what looks like an act of arbitrary distinction between matters of preservation and matters of morality, has he in his own way recognized the distinction between what were once called external goods and

goods of the soul; and in so doing, found a means for reconciling mechanical nature with both preservation and morality?
It is to the *Theory of Moral Sentiments* that one must turn for an
answer. The metaphor of the invisible hand serves its chief
theoretical purpose, I believe, in bringing to light a problem
for which the solution must be sought in a different context, as
I shall now attempt to show.

A leading question of the *Theory of Moral Sentiments* is,
What is virtue? Smith makes it clear from the outset that he is
in fact interested in the question, what are the grounds of the
distinction between right and wrong, what accounts for the
human recognition of this distinction and what accounts for
the large measure of practical respect enjoyed by the distinction? He begins his discussion – in the first sentence of the
book – by announcing a premise that will bear the weight of
much of what follows: "How selfish soever man may be supposed, there are evidently some principles in his nature which
interest him in the fortune of others, and render their happiness necessary to him, though he derives nothing from it but
the pleasure of seeing it." This is simply a matter of fact. But
Smith notes the further fact that there is no way by which one
human being can feel the feelings of another, although our
responding to those feelings plays so large a part in our lives.
The link that proves to join one sentient being to another is
imagination. We are forever having vicarious experiences
because we are able, indeed because we are unable not to
imagine ourselves in the other man's position. On the fact that
men, so to speak, exchange themselves in imagination with
one another depends the fact and the force of morality. One
observes a human act and one puts oneself, in imagination, in
the place of the agent, and, if there is a patient, then in his
place too. Then one considers whether there is a harmony
between the strength of the passion that moved the actor to act
and what one oneself could have felt in the same case. One
judges by the same means whether the gratitude or resentment of the patient was suitable to the good or ill received.
Thus human beings come to know approbation and disapprobation; but only because, through imagination, the feelings of
one man are transferred to another. The natural mechanism

that produces this transfer is responsible, therefore, for what is called Sympathy – a term that Smith insists be understood in the technical sense of fellow-feeling ("com-passion") rather than in the special sense of kindliness or benevolence: it applies to all the sentiments, gentle or angry.

The mere operation of the sympathy mechanism does not of itself explain morality, although it explains the approbation that underlies morality. In order to arrive at a norm that is undistorted by idiosyncrasy in bestowing and withholding approbation, Smith applies the construct of the Impartial Spectator, an imaginary bearer of the judgment of universal mankind which is infallible because of its impartiality as distinguished from its possible wisdom or virtue. If it be asked how any man can divine the judgment of the Impartial Spectator, the answer is that the Impartial Spectator is really none other than that "reason, principle, conscience, the inhabitant of the breast, the man within, the great judge and arbiter of our conduct."[4] We can easily enough find the way to duty by the use of natural common sense in conjunction with an honest desire to do right.[5] A man who forms his behavior on such lines will find by repeated experience that he gains the approbation not only of an imagined Impartial Spectator but of his living fellow men. He will find at the same time that he has discovered morality, for virtue is precisely what deserves the impartial approbation of humanity.

Smith sets it forth that men by nature desire or need the approbation of their fellows. We have by nature the strongest desire for the love, the gratitude, the admiration of mankind.[6] From this irresistible inclination proceed not only the general rules of morality but their strong grip on our behavior. Smith does not neglect the demands of preservation and utility; but he persistently denies that moral criteria or incentives can be derived from or reduced to considerations of mere advantage. Nature apparently does two things for mankind: it implants a

---

4   *Theory of Moral Sentiments*, Pt. III, Ch. III, p. 137.
5   Ibid., Pt. III, Ch. VI, p. 176.
6   Ibid., Pt. III, Ch. IV, p. 159.

powerful instinct of survival in the individual, even a tendency to gross and repellent selfishness; and it endows him with
the imagination and gregariousness that unite the species
mechanically through Sympathy. With the use of an invisible
hand, it cajoles and compels us to society and virtue, to prosperity and humanity.

Smith's work demonstrates that, if one takes nature quite
seriously and receives it altogether in its modern acceptation
as mechanism encompassing mankind, one need not reject as
a premise the impulsive sociality of man, or jeopardize morality, abandon mankind to deductions from self-preservation, or
jettison the virtues as such. Obviously it must be asked
whether an author may reasonably load or overload nature
with this philanthropic freight. We cannot reach that sovereign
question in this discussion, but must confine ourselves to the
meaning of Smith's project as a project.

Smith's thought is an impressive effort to solve, within the
limits of mechanical nature alone, the problem of morality: the
source and the ground of the distinction between right and
wrong, virtue and vice. It is a peculiarity of Smith's doctrine
that it resolves the central moral questions faithfully to the
tacit presupposition that nature is indeed the *comprehensive*
mechanism. Smith reasons by abstraction from the question of
man's freedom within the grip of that mechanism. Of course
he perceives that men are free to do well or ill, to heed or to
ignore the call of conscience. But that fact does not respond to
the much more radical question of freedom within nature, as
is clear from a formulation of the issue that directly addresses
Smith's own argument: Is the man who fulfills all the requirements of virtue as the sympathy mechanism defines virtue
preeminently free or preeminently a slave to the strong need
that men have for the approbation of their fellows? Evidently,
Smith does not regard this as a crucial question. If one had to
guess why he did not attach the importance to it that, for
example, Kant did, one might conjecture that he regarded the
difficulty as artificial or superfluous. For if one speaks literally of nature as comprehensive, as all-inclusive; and of man as
absolutely articulated in the chain of natural mechanism, then
one ought not to speak of man's bondage to or in nature, for

bondage is a relation between a one and some other which is capable of being "over against" the first. Two things may both be conceived as included in some larger One that comprehends them; and then either might be "over against" in relation to the other. But so far as the one is contained in the other as a part is in some whole, "bondage" is a misleading figure for characterizing the status of the part, for there is no "over against" in their relation. A wheel in a clock is not in bondage to the clock any more than the clock is in bondage to the wheel. Thus the question of man's "freedom" in the order of nature (under the stated assumptions of comprehensiveness and mechanism) does not arise spontaneously, i.e., without stimulation from presuppositions. It expresses the notion that to be part of *the* Whole is not different in principle from being part of any limited whole like a family or a city; and in seeing inclusion as assimilated to domination, it appears to envision subjection of the will of the part to the will of the whole. But precisely if the principle of the whole (nature, in this case) is mechanism – say the motion of lifeless matter according to mere laws of physics – then will can enter only as a confusing metaphor, and the issue of freedom is a gratuitous intrusion in the context. It is in a sense such as this that the difficulty could be regarded as artificial or superfluous. I freely grant that Smith's references to the intention of nature appear to expose him to the charge that he imputes a will to nature. Those references would have to be shown very precisely to point to some characteristic of nature that differs decisively from volition, in order for Smith's abstraction from the question of freedom vis-à-vis nature to be adequately covered by the suggested reasoning. For the immediate purpose, I am assuming, but cannot discuss the assumption, that a purely mechanical principle such as that of evolution through natural selection is compatible with a teleology of nature but does not presuppose a will in nature.

Superfluously to raise the question of man's bondage to nature has effects that go beyond the theoretical. It either prepares the way for despair: there is no escape from the absolutely comprehensive and equally tyrannical grip of the natural All; or it compels men to find, which probably means invent, an enclave inside or a platform outside nature in the form of a state of the consciousness or the will, by which in spirit man will elevate himself to freedom in a sense most elusive. (I speak profanely, of course, and without respect to what may be hoped for through the enlightenment of revelation.)

Articulating man entirely within nature, yet declining to see a question of man's freedom vis-à-vis nature, Smith has adopted an ancient simplicity: man's integration in the order of nature is beneficial rather than threatening to humanity, and is concordant with man's sociality and his virtue. Smith's project for liberal commercial society is part of his wider project for accommodating man's sociality and morality to the environment of mechanistic nature, although the traditional setting for that conception of man in nature is the older and teleological vision of nature. Evaluations of commercial liberalism that do not consider this fact are, I believe, to that extent defective. And they deprive one, moreover, of access to a most interesting reflection: modern society, like modern natural science, might be more reconcilable with the moral benefits that we tend to connect with "the tradition" than we sometimes permit ourselves to perceive.

Perhaps the time has come to remind ourselves of the twin bicentennial with which we began. Through reflection on the issues that surround the concept of the invisible hand, we are enabled to see what justifies Smith in restricting the sense of the term "liberty" to contexts that must be called social or political, and thus what allows him to use such an expression as "natural liberty" without internal contradiction. If we see so much, we may see also the superfluousness of the vast and popular constructions that presuppose the bondage of man in nature, and deduce on that foundation ambitious projects for an imaginary human emancipation that have carried great masses of mankind into very palpable political servitude. Finally, we may see the sense in which the *Wealth Of Nations* illuminates the liberal commercial polity of the United States, vindicating it at least in part against those moral complaints that arise from insufficient thought about freedom in and out of nature.

INDEX